D1459851

Investing in Entrepreneurs

Investing in Entrepreneurs

A Strategic Approach for Strengthening Your Regional and Community Economy

Gregg A. Lichtenstein and Thomas S. Lyons

 PRAEGER

AN IMPRINT OF ABC-CLIO, LLC
Santa Barbara, California • Denver, Colorado • Oxford, England

Library of Congress Cataloging-in-Publication Data

Lichtenstein, Gregg A.
   Investing in entrepreneurs : a strategic approach for strengthening your regional and community economy / Gregg A. Lichtenstein and Thomas S. Lyons.
       p. cm.
   Includes bibliographical references and index.
   ISBN 978-0-313-38292-5 (alk. paper) — ISBN 978-0-313-38293-2 (ebook)
1. Entrepreneurship.   2. Economic development.   3. Industrial promotion.   4. New business enterprises.   5. Regional planning.
I. Lyons, Thomas S.   II. Title.
   HB615.L493   2010
   658.4'21—dc22   2010021213

ISBN: 978-0-313-38292-5

EISBN: 978-0-313-38293-2

14   13   12   11   10   1   2   3   4   5

This book is also available on the World Wide Web as an eBook.
Visit www.abc-clio.com for details.

Praeger
An Imprint of ABC-CLIO, LLC

ABC-CLIO, LLC
130 Cremona Drive, P.O. Box 1911
Santa Barbara, California 93116-1911

This book is printed on acid-free paper ∞

Manufactured in the United States of America

Contents

Acknowledgments

Along the path of the 25-year journey we have taken to writing this book, we have had the privilege of working with many individuals who have influenced our thinking and enriched our understanding. These people are too numerous to acknowledge individually; instead, we would like to extend a blanket thank you to the hundreds of entrepreneurs and dozens of entrepreneurship assistance professionals with whom we have interacted over the years. You have our unflagging respect and admiration, and your insights are deeply appreciated.

There are a few individuals to whom we owe special thanks, however. We want to express our deep gratitude to Gary Perkins and Keith Rabalais, general manager and former general manager, respectively, of the Entrepreneurial League System® of Central Louisiana for their vision, dedication, wisdom, and tireless effort in working with us to develop the skills of entrepreneurs. We thank Mark Burdette, former general manager of the Advantage Valley Entrepreneurial League System®, for his pioneering efforts in putting our ideas to work in the field. Jim Hurst's assistance in analyzing performance data was invaluable, as was his entrepreneur coaching work in Central Louisiana. In fact, we owe a debt of gratitude to all of the coaches, past and present, who have worked on the Entrepreneurial League System® projects. Their stories from the field have contributed significantly to this book.

Our understanding of entrepreneurship skills and how to identify and communicate them has been greatly enhanced by the insights of Charles Faulkner. Thanks also to Nailya Kutzhanova for acquainting us with the literature of skill building and helping us to apply it to entrepreneurial development.

We offer a special thank you to Ellen Lichtenstein for the untold hours of conversation, her sharp copyediting eye, and for not hesitating to tell us when the points we were trying to make failed to hit the mark. Many thanks to Brian Romer, our editor at ABC-CLIO/Praeger, to our publishing agent, Stan Wakefield, and to our graphic artist, Anne Bullen.

Introduction

If you want truly to understand something, try to change it.

—Kurt Lewin

THE CHALLENGE WE FACE

This book reflects a journey of more than 25 years, during which we have sought to answer the question: *How can we help entrepreneurs build successful businesses?*

This is not a theoretical question being asked by academics or armchair philosophers, but rather a real, practical question that challenges us, and everyone in the field of economic development, every day.

In addition to having launched and operated our own businesses and social ventures, we have had the privilege of working directly with more than 1,500 entrepreneurs on numerous long-term consulting engagements, strategic alliances, and counseling and coaching relationships. We've walked into businesses representing many different industries, markets, and locations—urban as well as rural. We have worked with high-tech and low-tech firms, service businesses as well as manufacturers, publicly held companies, family-held firms, and mom-and-pop shops. We've worked with entrepreneurs from different countries, vastly different cultures within the same country, from different races and ethnic groups, and from both genders. Many have had advanced degrees; some have never finished college.

But each time we come face-to-face with another entrepreneur, we wonder: How is this individual and his firm different than what we've seen before, and is this difference important? Everyone in the fields of education, medicine, sports—anyone dealing with real human beings—encounters this question every single day.

There are two classic approaches, representing the ends of a spectrum: we can choose to treat everyone the same or we can choose to treat everyone differently. The first option is efficient, because it ignores differences in favor of a one-size fits all solution, but it is not necessarily effective. The second option is effective because each solution is customized, but it is not efficient because it ignores similarities. There are dangers in both extremes. How do we decide what to do?

Usually we search for some kind of a criterion that will enable us to sort and categorize clients in useful ways. However, the traditional criteria we use to classify entrepreneurs—by their age, gender, location, type of business—are simply not helpful. These characteristics are superficial and do not reveal anything useful about their needs.

This problem became clear to us many years ago, when, as committee members for a major economic development trade association, we were called upon to conduct focus groups of business incubator managers. The association staff wanted to group the managers into those that deal with technology firms, those that managed programs in rural areas, those that operated empowerment incubators in the inner cities, and those that ran mixed-use incubators. Given our desire to achieve the greatest impact with the least amount of effort, we questioned this classification. The answer we got from the staff is that obviously (to them at least), technology entrepreneurs are very different from entrepreneurs that operate in rural and urban areas and had to be separated.

We were not trying to be uncooperative, but we couldn't see it. Entrepreneurs all have problems with obtaining financing, finding good workers, and the like, no matter where they lived or what industry they are in. We insisted on knowing what the real differences were; the distinctions that made a difference.

The fact is that the descriptors the association wanted to focus on don't capture anything of real value or importance. We knew there were significant differences among entrepreneurs and believed that substantive knowledge of them would enable us to be both efficient and effective in helping entrepreneurs build successful companies—if we could only discover what they were. So we set out to find a map of this territory. Failing to discover anything useful, we decided to create our own. This book describes that map and how to use it.

GUIDING PRINCIPLES

This map had to help us accomplish the following objectives:

1. To generate action-usable knowledge so that we can be both efficient and effective in our work with entrepreneurs
2. To act entrepreneurially
3. To build systemic solutions for individual entrepreneurs as well as the community of entrepreneurs
4. To produce transformational changes

These four goals served as guiding principles in our development of our map—which we call the Pipeline of Entrepreneurs and Enterprises.

Generate Action-Usable Knowledge

Our goal is to generate knowledge that works; in other words, knowledge that helps us and others to produce a consistently high level of performance in determining who the entrepreneur is, what they need, and how to help them.

To accomplish this, we needed to develop a theory about how this world operates. As Kurt Lewin explained, "there is nothing so practical as a good theory." But for our purposes, what makes a theory good?

As Cortlandt Cammann observed, "from the perspective of an agent of change, knowledge is not helpful unless it can be turned into *action* . . . having a theory that helped me to understand was not necessarily the same as having knowledge that could guide my action."[1] Why do Eskimos, for example, have so many different words for snow? It is because they *need* them for their survival; they *use* these distinctions to successfully navigate the world around them. Many ideas or concepts in entrepreneurship and economic development sound impressive, but when you attempt to implement them, you find they are incapable of being used or applied.

For us, a good theory must be capable of being "operationalized," that is, implemented. Its value lies in how effectively it guides our efforts and improves our results. At the same time, good theory is built from the ground up, on the basis of experience with what works and what doesn't. The generation of action-usable knowledge is a virtuous and continuous cycle, in which theory and practice are intimately linked.

4 *Investing in Entrepreneurs*

The knowledge presented in this book has not been abstractly generated by outside observers detached from the world of experience. These concepts and ideas are derived directly from our interactions as practitioners, both successful and unsuccessful, with entrepreneurs. Whatever wisdom this book offers reflects hard-won lessons working with the subjects of this book.

Act Entrepreneurially

But at the same time, we weren't simply acting as practitioners. To generate action-usable knowledge, one must engage in "action research." Action research involves not only developing ideas and concepts out of practice, but also testing those ideas in practice—not by conducting surveys but by implementing the idea directly with clients.[2]

For example, in a long-term project with over 150 inner-city manufacturing firms in Philadelphia, we had identified what we believed to be a pressing need for new product development. So we launched what proved to be a very successful initiative. We were later asked by an agency evaluating our work how we knew that these firms needed help with new product development. They specifically requested to see our survey results. We told them we hadn't done one. They were stunned. They wanted to know how we could make such a claim and argue that it was valid, without any survey results!

The proof of our claim was in the actions of the owners of the 17 manufacturing firms who participated in a monthly new product development initiative for a period of 24 months and developed new products, when none of them had been doing any product development before. In other words, it is because of what they did, rather than what they said, that we drew the conclusions we did.

How did we *know* it was going to work before we launched our new product development initiative? Frankly, we didn't, and that didn't matter to us. You see, we are skeptical of research that relies on people's words or espousals, rather than their actual behavior. It is commonplace for people to say one thing and to do another. For example, very few people admit to buying and reading the *National Enquirer,* yet their paid circulation is over 2.5 million people. We avoid the conflict between words and deeds by concerning ourselves less about what people say and more about what they do.[3] By acting as entrepreneurs, rather than as traditional academic researchers, we started with a project launch instead of a survey.

In this situation, we had gotten to know these manufacturers well. We had observed their circumstances carefully over time and could see the need clearly. So we felt our conclusion had a certain qualitative rather than quantitative validity, grounded as it was in our interactions with these clients. Most importantly, we were willing to take a calculated risk to test our ideas in practice, first.

The process we followed started with in-depth engagement and experience with a set of clients over a couple of years. This led to forming a "hypothesis" about the need for new products, which then led us to test that hypothesis by making an actual offering to the clients in order to determine if the need was real. It cost us nothing to make the offer (marketing research costs were close to zero). We were more than willing to design and implement it quickly, if we received a favorable reception.

This sequence of activities is quite different from the more traditional market research process in which someone comes up with an idea (all too frequently without interacting with any live clients), goes out and tests that idea using a survey instrument or focus group, and then launches a new offering or initiative on the basis of the findings.

Not only does that lead to a lot of false positives (we are constantly advising our less sophisticated clients not to launch a new business on the basis of the expressed willingness of their friends and families to buy their product), it is also extremely time-consuming and inefficient. In the fast-paced world of business, we don't have that kind of cycle time to find answers and achieve results. The process must be reengineered.

Admittedly it takes courage to face clients with ideas that may or may not be fully formed and to get shot down (we stopped counting how many times that has happened). But invariably two valuable things occur in that process: we get the honest feedback we need to improve our ideas, and we make friends who are also interested in learning along with us. This approach contrasts starkly with the "expert" model, where the expert, who is rarely wrong, speaks and everyone else simply listens.

By not trying to figure it all out in advance, by being willing to be wrong and then change what we were doing on the basis of what was being learned during the implementation process, we were engaging in continuous improvement. We took advantage of every opportunity to experiment responsibly, which means to make mistakes with limited downside or negative impact for our clients as well as ourselves. The result was that over time, we couldn't help but get better at what we were doing.

Build Solutions That Are Systemic

There is a tendency in the economic development field, as in many others, to search for the Holy Grail or magic bullet—the one solution that will solve all problems. Such point solutions, as we call them, are an illusion. They are partial and, while useful, they cannot possibly work by themselves, in isolation. Point solutions simply don't include all of the ingredients necessary for success. We must face the truth that the days when a single approach will solve every problem are over (if in fact there ever was such a time).

A championship in football is not guaranteed simply by having a great quarterback. Quarterbacks need receivers to throw to, offensive linemen to protect the quarterback from the defensive rush, and people to defend against the offense of the other team and kickers. In other words, there are many ingredients required for success. Although some may be relatively more important than others, there is no single ingredient that, when taken alone, will guarantee victory. And the same reality exists in entrepreneurship and economic development.

We must work to ensure not only that we have all of the ingredients in a comprehensive solution, but also that these ingredients work together to produce a result (a whole) that is greater than the sum of its parts. This is the essence of a system.

Another sports example provides an illustration of what we mean by a system. Why is it that an all-star team is rarely able to beat a championship team? Clearly an all-star team has better talent at each of the positions. But it is the relationship or chemistry among the players that is the key to the success of the championship team—they know how to *play together.*

Chemistry matters, which is why managers and coaches are always looking for the right player to put in their lineup that will catalyze the team to a level of performance that will take them to a championship. Oftentimes, that player is not the "star" or even the best player on the team in terms of her individual skills. But it is her fit with the other players and the response she commands from members of the team that makes the difference. In other words, it is the relationships among the elements that make a system more than the sum of the parts. While we are utilizing sports examples to make this point because they are widely understood, this observation is valid for any collective endeavor, like theater groups, jazz ensembles and, most germane to this book, businesses.

Building systemic solutions requires that we begin to deal with the complexity in the world rather than to avoid it. Obvious as the previous examples may seem to be, most economic development solutions fail to meet these two criteria for building systemic solutions: including all of the necessary ingredients and making sure that the ingredients fit together well into a recipe. This problem occurs on an individual basis when we fail to treat the entrepreneur as a whole, and at a societal level when we fail to treat the community as a whole by focusing exclusively on one part of the population and ignoring the rest.

In terms of individual entrepreneurs, "the issue is that business problems are complex and multi-dimensional. They are not always amenable to a simple, single solution nor are they exclusively financial, marketing, managerial or operational in nature. At best, specialized approaches tend to produce partial solutions; in the worst cases, they contribute to the failure of the firm by doing the right things, but in the wrong order."[4]

On the community level, we all too often practice a form of monoculture, with an exclusive focus on technology entrepreneurs or "high-impact" clients or growth firms, as if the others are irrelevant to our economies or not worthy from a cost–benefit point of view. We question this assumption.[5] We can no longer measure the health of the larger economic whole from the condition of its favorite part. We cannot assume that if I am personally doing well, then the whole economy must be doing well. We cannot assume that the economic splits between the haves and have-nots will be reduced by trickle-up or trickle-down flows, without paying attention to the reality—a world in which these changes are not happening like the fairy tale promised.

We need a system that does not just help one segment of the population and exclude the rest. We cannot afford more solutions in which I win at your expense, or you win at mine. Too many of our systems have been set up this way, and they are undermining the trust on which every functioning economy is built. We can and must do better.

To help satisfy this requirement, our map needs to give us the ability to look at the population of entrepreneurs in our communities or regions as a whole *and* as a set of parts, so that we can see the relationship of all the parts to the whole. In this highly interdependent age we live in, such a framework will help us create solutions that are synergistic or win/win.

Produce Transformational Changes

We want a map that will enable us to produce transformational changes. This means fundamentally increasing the capacity of both the individual entrepreneurs as well as the entire entrepreneurial community to deal with new circumstances and achieve their goals. A fundamental change in one's abilities involves making a substantial improvement; it is not about being incremental. We are not referring to someone changing their batting average from .250 to .255—an increase of 2 percent. Instead, the changes we seek to produce involve taking their performance to another, entirely different, much higher level of competitive play.

The best way to explain this kind of change is to describe a classification of economic offerings developed by Pine and Gilmore. According to these management thinkers, there is a hierarchy among five types of economic offerings—commodities, goods, services, experiences, and transformations—based upon the value they add (see Figure 1).[6] At the base of this hierarchy are commodities, which are distinguished from one another only by price. At the next step of the hierarchy are physical goods, which offer greater value by presenting different features or benefits. Additional value is added by services; however, their intangible nature makes it more difficult to assess this value and compare it to like offerings.

Increasingly, consumers are demanding offerings that cannot be adequately described by these first three categories. The next level of offering "occurs when a company intentionally uses goods as props and services as the stage for engaging the customer in such a way that creates a memorable event."[7] The offering is "no longer the goods or services themselves, but the experiences they create." Examples can be drawn from enterprises such as Disney World to eating establishments like Planet Hollywood.

Experiences, however, are not the highest level of economic offerings. "Just as customizing a good automatically turns it into a service, so customizing an experience turns it into something distinct. If you

FIGURE 1.
Hierarchy of Economic Offerings

Transformations

Experiences

Services

Goods

Commodities

Source: B. J. Pine II and J. H. Gilmore, *The Experience Economy* (Boston: Harvard Business School Press, 1999).

design an experience so in tune with what an individual needs at an exact juncture in time, you cannot help but change that individual—guiding him to (and through) a life-transforming experience."[8] Transformations add the most value of all of the economic offerings in the hierarchy.

Experiences and transformations are not just another kind of service. "Both goods and services exist completely outside the recipient . . . the new economic offerings . . . are inherently personal. . . . Experiences only occur within the individual, while transformations go even further and actually change the individual buyer . . . experiences unfold over a duration of time and transformations must be sustained through time."[9]

The evolution of the business incubation concept provides an illustration of how these five types of offerings differ. When incubators were first introduced, their principal offering was low-cost (below-market) space, a commodity that added value only through its price. Soon, incubator developers and managers realized that value could be added to the space by creating "goods" such as shared resources, flexible leasing terms, and work areas that could be tailored to the needs of individual client entrepreneurs. The next stage in their evolution saw incubators offering business services such as business planning, marketing, and operations assistance, which added intangible value. Most recently, incubators have recognized the benefits of the experiences provided by bringing entrepreneurs together in one program, including information sharing, moral support, and opportunities for creating business partnerships.[10]

The highest level of economic offering would be to help entrepreneurs develop skills in building successful companies; in other words, to guide entrepreneurial transformations.[11] Transformations are not achieved by adding up individual service transactions; a much more systemic approach is required (such as the new kind of offering to be discussed in this book). Partial solutions are no longer enough. Our times demand more fundamental and transformational changes.

Yes, this is idealistic, but it is driven by a practical idealism. Our goal is to figure out what it takes to implement these ideals, not to satisfy ourselves with dreams and visions (and glossy reports on those dreams and visions). The true test is: does it work?

OUR INNOVATION

The Pipeline of Entrepreneurs (and Enterprises) is a map, as well as a process of mapping that enables us to differentiate among entrepreneurs and enterprises. It gives us a more effective means of segmenting our market or customer base so that we can improve our performance in helping entrepreneurs build successful companies.

The field today is filled with numerous answers to the question about how to help entrepreneurs become more successful: increase venture capital funding, make more bank loans, provide more technical assistance, encourage entrepreneurs to take business planning courses, provide them with marketing information, establish more incubation programs, and so on.

But these suggestions are all tool-based; they lead with the means—a service or offering—and not the ends to which we are working. What we are left wondering is, how can we know what to offer, until or unless we know who the entrepreneurs are and what they need? This then becomes the first and most fundamental question: *who are the entrepreneurs and how does who they are determine how we can best help them build successful companies?*

Our map, or Pipeline, will facilitate the next step in the evolution of this field by shifting the primary focus from the tools to the entrepreneurs. This does not mean we are no longer concerned with tools or should ignore what we have learned to date. It only means that we change our emphasis: we place tools in the service of the entrepreneurs. In other words, market demand should drive the supply of support and assistance, rather than the suppliers of the tools determining what help entrepreneurs receive.

The Pipeline will enable the economic development field to advance from being tool-centered to being client-centered. When one's only tool is a hammer, everything begins to look like nails. A tool-centered orientation causes its users to think and act locally in their own interests rather than in the interest of the whole, because they cannot even see the whole. Using the Pipeline as a map does not require the user to give up his hammer; it enables him to use it more appropriately—in the right circumstances with the right clients to greater effect. It enables the suppliers of tools to view the market more holistically and, as a result, to act more globally. In an increasingly complex world, this change in behavior will take our efforts to the next level.

In evaluating this book, we ask you to judge it by its usefulness in enabling you to:

- Generate action-usable knowledge in order to be both efficient and effective in your work with entrepreneurs
- Act entrepreneurially
- Build solutions for individual entrepreneurs as well as the community of entrepreneurs that are systemic
- Produce transformational changes

THE FLOW OF THE BOOK

In this book, we seek to reframe the discussion about economic development and how it should be pursued. We make the case for economic development that is entrepreneur-centered and focused on development, as opposed to growth. We introduce and explicate our framework for making this happen—the Pipeline of Entrepreneurs and Enterprises. We demonstrate how the Pipeline can be used to address common economic development challenges in systemic, systematic, and strategic ways, and we lay out the basic principles for Pipeline-guided development.

We start in chapter 1 by asserting the crucial role of entrepreneurs in economic development past, present, and future. We make the claim that entrepreneurs and their contributions have been largely ignored in recent decades and that they must be reinserted into the economic development arena. Finally, we reframe economic development as managing the community's portfolio of entrepreneurs and enterprises.

Chapter 2 examines the concept of development, what it actually means, and why it is crucial to true economic development. This chapter argues against the current practices of economic development that focus on growth, as these are scalar and have no power to transform local and regional economies.

In chapters 3 and 4, we explore the two key variables that make up the Pipeline—entrepreneurial skill levels and business life cycle stages, respectively. Chapter 3 provides a detailed discussion of why and how entrepreneurs should be distinguished by their skill level, while chapter 4 delineates a model of the stages in the business life cycle that permits clear differentiation between stages and facilitates strategic business development interventions at each stage. We put these two dimensions together, in chapter 5, to form a Pipeline that enables a community to map its entrepreneurial assets. We show how to produce various mappings that provide detailed knowledge about the composition of assets in the community.

Chapter 6 explores the relationship between entrepreneurial skills and the business life cycle and examines the dynamics they produce. In chapter 7, we detail the economic development strategies needed to manage the Pipeline and how to evaluate them. Then, in chapter 8, we present a series of scenarios familiar to economic developers, break them down using the Pipeline, and discuss options for developing strategic solutions to the challenges these scenarios present.

Chapter 9 pulls all of the preceding knowledge together into a set of guiding principles that economic developers should use in managing their community's or region's Pipeline. Finally, chapter 10 offers some concluding remarks.

WHO THIS BOOK IS FOR

This book will benefit anyone whose role is to encourage or promote entrepreneurship in their company, community, or region. In particular, we want to reach out to entrepreneurs who are in a position to take leadership roles within their communities on economic development issues.

This book will also benefit anyone who works with entrepreneurs and businesses. The Pipeline will help equity investors as well as bankers to better understand the dynamics of their investments. It will help firms that provide professional services to businesses of all kinds— accountants, lawyers, and marketing/communications specialists, as well as human resource providers—to know who their clients are, what their needs are, and what challenges they are facing. Similarly, it will benefit practitioners and policymakers in the nonprofit and public sectors who have a role in providing assistance to entrepreneurs. If you need a better understanding of your marketplace, if you want to improve the effectiveness and efficiency of your services to entrepreneurs, this book will be invaluable.

This book will also be useful to students of economic development and community development and who are examining the relationship between these fields and entrepreneurship. Finally, if you are an economic developer who is exploring whether or not to include entrepreneurship in your plans, who is not sure how to help entrepreneurs or what your role should be, you will find plenty of help in this book in thinking through the answers to those questions.

1

Rediscovering Our Roots: Entrepreneurs and Entrepreneurship Leading Economic Development

Most new jobs won't come from our biggest employers. They will come from our smallest. We've got to do everything we can to make entrepreneurial dreams a reality.

—Ross Perot

Entrepreneurs are the true heroes of the U.S. economy. By identifying viable business opportunities, assembling the resources and expertise required for pursuit of those opportunities, and successfully managing the growth process, they have continuously created the collective business assets that constitute this country's economic portfolio. Through the process of "creative destruction" that characterizes innovation,[1] they continually refresh our economy and keep it globally competitive.

To be sure, "rock-star-level" entrepreneurs, like Bill Gates, Steve Jobs, and Sam Walton, have received their share of media attention and public adulation; however, this attention did not come until they had created large, highly visible companies. Meanwhile, most entrepreneurs are underappreciated and labor in relative obscurity. As a nation, we seem to have collectively forgotten from where the large corporations that are our central focus of attention came. These corporations did not spring from the earth fully formed. They are the later-stage products of a long-term entrepreneurial process that began in someone's garage or basement. They are the culmination of an individual's vision for building wealth.

We have become overly dependent on these corporations for employment, research and development, public finance, and community and

nation building. Now, as they shrink, consolidate, or disappear, we find
that our old models of economic development, which were based on
the nurturing of these corporations in exchange for growth in jobs and
tax base, are obsolete. Ironically, we find ourselves turning our attention
back to entrepreneurship as the source of the small, nimble companies
that can navigate the difficult waters of the global economy. Even as we
do so, however, our approach to entrepreneurship-focused economic development is highly fragmented and localized. It is largely spearheaded
by public and nonprofit organizations that have no real understanding
of entrepreneurship and whose structure is bureaucratic and, therefore,
antithetical to the ways of entrepreneurship. Entrepreneurs—the people
who best understand entrepreneurship and who are most likely to be
able to help society in this regard—have been left out of the economic
development mix. They not only should be involved, they should be
leading the charge.

   This chapter explains how we came to this point and what we should
do about it. It examines who entrepreneurs are; what their historical
role has been in economic development; how that has changed and why;
and why it is important for entrepreneurs to reinsert themselves in the
economic development process. The chapter concludes by introducing
a useful way for reframing economic development that puts entrepreneurship at its heart.

WHO IS AN ENTREPRENEUR?

Entrepreneurship is a word, like so many in the English language, that has
been abused to the point that it is in danger of becoming meaningless.[2]
In many elite business schools, it is so narrowly defined as to include
only the activities of businesspeople who build high growth, venture
capital-backed "gazelle" (to use David Birch's term) companies. Social
service organizations and the private foundations that support them
have co-opted the term for their social agendas to a degree that jeop-
ardizes its connection to business at all. Public policy theorists and
policymakers would have us believe that entrepreneurship is nothing
more than a mindset that can be fostered through education and public "cheerleading." Each of these viewpoints is myopic and dangerous,
in the sense that the whole of entrepreneurship is lost, thus dimin-
ishing the opportunity to utilize this powerful force for transforming
economies.

While there are numerous definitions of entrepreneurship from which to choose, our preferred definition comes from the economist Burton Klein, who stated that an entrepreneur is "a marriage broker between what is desirable from an economic point of view and what is possible from a technological (i.e., operational) point of view."[3]

We like this definition for several reasons. First, it is broad enough to include the activities of a wide variety of entrepreneurs, not merely those who run gazelle firms and not just those who start new companies, but those who revitalize existing firms as well. Second, it remains firmly rooted in the term's business origins. Third, it alludes to the fact that entrepreneurship is not merely a mindset, but a process with a clear end product. Finally, it characterizes entrepreneurs as people who help to make economic dreams come true—people with a vision for adding value to our lives, who have the leadership skills to rally other people around their vision, and who are willing to manage the risks inherent in launching or rebuilding an enterprise for pursuing that vision.[4]

THE HISTORICAL ROLE OF ENTREPRENEURS IN ECONOMIC DEVELOPMENT

Entrepreneurs have been directly involved in building the U.S. economy since before the American Revolution. As artisans, shopkeepers, and early industrialists, many of whom introduced innovations and grew their businesses around them, they anchored and developed that economy. Their individual business decisions and their active participation in local governance constituted early economic development.

As one example, Hashikawa notes that rural entrepreneurs in New Jersey in the colonial period took advantage of their access to natural resources and to large urban markets in New York and Philadelphia to create small enterprises in such industries as flour milling and iron making. These ventures were limited by the inability of their entrepreneurs to go beyond their immediate locale for resources, which caused business failure when the resources were exhausted; however, they represent an early step toward the regionally, nationally, and globally integrated companies of today's economy.[5]

It has been argued that William Penn, the founder of the Pennsylvania colony, was an early social and political entrepreneur. Penn sought to protect the religious and individual freedoms of Quakers in his colony. He recognized, in order to accomplish that objective, that he needed to create a system that guaranteed the same freedoms to all groups. This social invention was made manifest in the Charter of Pennsylvania. In doing this, he also created a freer, less regulated economic environment relative to other colonies.[6]

Another example of colonial-era entrepreneurship comes from the then thriving whaling industry. The people of the island of Nantucket recognized an opportunity when sperm whales were discovered living in deeper waters than had traditionally been hunted. It was very difficult to tow these large animals to shore in order to process them for oil, and it was too expensive to chunk the whale blubber and bring it back to shore to be rendered. Thus, Nantucket, led by entrepreneur Joseph Starbuck, began manufacturing larger whaling ships designed for both hunting the whales and processing them at sea. This also served to allow whalers to stay at sea longer. The whaling industry had been revolutionized.[7]

Well-known entrepreneurs of the period of the American Revolution included Benjamin Franklin, George Mason, and Robert Morris. In the early 1800s, Robert Fulton introduced steamboat travel. By 1850, Samuel Morris's telegraph was in wide use.[8] All of these entrepreneurs contributed dramatically to the economy and quality of life of the first 75 years of the United States of America.

Evans, exploring the role of entrepreneurship in the economic development of the United States between 1850 and 1954, describes entrepreneurs as "men of action," who used their understanding of the importance of timing and changes in society to advance development.[9] This suggests an entrepreneur who not only understood business, but was attuned to his community and world as well. This was an entrepreneur who was directly involved in economic development, not as a player whose actions are manipulated by others, but as one whose knowledge and understanding permit him to manipulate the economy to his benefit and that of his community.

WHAT CHANGED AND WHY IS IT A PROBLEM?

While entrepreneurs continued to play an important role in the U.S. economy and its development, their role became increasingly overshadowed by those of big business and big government. The fruits of entrepreneurs' labors yielded large numbers of big regional and national companies and global corporations over the years. They became major employers. They paid large sums in taxes. Their huge advertising budgets kept their names in front of the general public, and their large research and development (R&D) budgets put them at the center of new product creation. Business became synonymous with the corporation. Because of their clout, these corporations became the darlings of government economic developers, who sought to woo and placate them as a strategy. While small business people typically had to fight for everything they got from government, support for corporations came much more easily. We had entered the era of corporatism and "corporate welfare."

For a large portion of the period in history between about 1850 and 1900, the power and influence of the "captains of industry" was much greater than that of government. This was the era of the Industrial Revolution and laissez faire (a policy in which government was expected to "keep its hands off" business). Warner called this approach "privatism"—business was to take the lead in developing the economy, and government was to act as a referee in the case of disputes.[10]

With the rise of the Progressives at the turn of the 21st century came the professionalization of government and the demise of the corrupt "political machines" that sprang up in the era of privatism. This set the stage for what would happen after the Panic of 1929, which resulted in the Great Depression. During this period, the public lost faith in business and its seeming infallibility. With Roosevelt's New Deal, government became the savior of the economy and grew to unprecedented size and strength. Among the societal duties previously held by business that governments assumed was economic development. Governments largely continue to handle this duty today.

World War II and its aftermath reestablished the economy and the place of the large corporation in it. Entrepreneurs remained the nameless, faceless backbone of the economy. Government dictated economic development policy. During this period, businesspeople focused on their businesses, leaving governance to government. A separation of labor emerged in this regard. Unfortunately, this situation left people in charge of economic development who had little or no business knowledge and absolutely no idea of what it takes to be a successful entrepreneur, nor any appreciation for why that might be important. It also created businesspeople who were removed from governance, without the time or interest to pursue it. Economic-development-related public policy became narrowly defined as that which impacts corporate interests, and lobbyists became business's chief policy influencers. Most economic development policy reflects all of these elements to this day.

This situation has upset the original homeostasis of private/public interaction, taking it from seamless to siloed and adversarial. Government has become an entity removed from those it governs, and business has become a member of society that must be either bribed or forced to do what is in the best interests of that society. This is not universally true, of course, but it is true across a broad enough spectrum to make it a major problem. Each sector is doing "its job," but neither is doing a very good job of moving society forward. Where are those early entrepreneurs who built personal and community wealth, while being active in the governance of their locales? Where are these men and women who were not so specialized that they were unable see the whole, the interconnections, the tapestry of society?

WHY ENTREPRENEURS MUST REINSERT THEMSELVES IN ECONOMIC DEVELOPMENT

If this country is to reassert its economic dominance and protect its quality of life, we need to rediscover our economic roots. We need to acknowledge the singular importance of entrepreneurship to our economic strength. We need to once again engage entrepreneurs in governance. We also need to make entrepreneurship the focus of our economic development efforts and trust entrepreneurs to lead in this arena.

This will not happen, however, if the current system is left to its own devices. That will only ensure inertia. Entrepreneurs must make the case for themselves and not rely on others to do it for them. They must reestablish themselves in the mainstream of American economic and public life. This can happen when entrepreneurs come together in their communities and regions; when they become a "community of entrepreneurs."

MANAGING THE COMMUNITY'S PORTFOLIO OF ENTREPRENEURS AND THEIR ENTERPRISES

Arguably, entrepreneurship takes place at every stage in a business's life cycle. By starting and building a business around an opportunity that adds value to customers, by revitalizing a declining company, by spinning a new enterprise out of a mature firm, or by successfully taking a new technology to market, entrepreneurs make substantial contributions to their communities' economies. The collective efforts of these entrepreneurs accounts for an enormous portion of our economy. In fact, when viewed as the driving force behind the progression of a company through the stages in the life cycle that exists in every industry, entrepreneurship becomes the basis for all economic activity in any given community or region.

The numbers on the impact of entrepreneurship on the economy are impressive, and these are derived using a much narrower definition of entrepreneurship than the one employed in this book. According to the U.S. Small Business Administration's Office of Advocacy, companies with 500 or fewer employees account for 99 percent of all employers and 75 percent of new jobs.[11] These businesses also account for about 50 percent of total sales and of gross domestic product (GDP).[12] "Gazelle" companies—firms that grow at an annual rate of 20 percent or more for four consecutive years and constitute only 3 percent of all companies—generated five million jobs in the period 1994–98.[13] Furthermore, small businesses produce about 55 percent of all new innovations.[14]

All of this suggests that entrepreneurship is worthy of our collective attention as a nation. The many entrepreneurial ventures that make up our economy are business assets of varying and complementary types. These combined assets constitute this country's wealth base. It is a portfolio of assets, which must be catalogued and managed if it is to achieve a maximum yield.

Yet, we are not thinking about our entrepreneurial assets in this way, when we think about them at all. Our knowledge of these assets is superficial and incomplete. We may be able to add up numbers of companies in our communities, but we know little or nothing about the quality of those companies or the entrepreneurs behind them. As a consequence, we are woefully ignorant of the skill level of our entrepreneurs or the stage in the life cycle of their businesses at any given point in time. What information we do have is fragmented, categorical, incomplete, and largely irrelevant to the task at hand. How does one manage a portfolio of assets with this kind of information? As a result, we waste resources and miss opportunities at every turn.

The essence of economic development in the 21st century should be the management of our regional portfolios of entrepreneurial assets across the country. We should know precisely what is in each portfolio, where there are gaps, where the portfolio is weak, and where it is strong. Then, just as a money market portfolio manager does, we should develop and implement strategies to address weaknesses, leverage strengths, and balance investments to ensure long-term success. In economic development, this means using our tools of intervention (e.g., business incubation, microenterprise development, equity capital investment, tax incentives, land write-downs, etc.) systemically, systematically, and strategically to protect and enhance our entrepreneurial assets with a goal of transforming the economy of the given region.[15] Just as importantly, it means involving entrepreneurs in these efforts—as advisors, strategists, implementers, and leaders. The remainder of this book is about how to do this.

2

Putting "Development" Back into Economic Development

Without development there is no profit, without profit no development. For the capitalist system it must be added further that without profit there would be no accumulation of wealth.

—Joseph Schumpeter

Somewhere along the way, economic development has become less about development and more about growth. Growth, itself, is not necessarily a bad thing, but it is very limited. It is about creating more of something and does not address the issue of quality. At essence it is scalar. It is rooted in the assumption common to the American culture that more is better. Yet more of anything does not necessarily guarantee its quality.

Most economic development activities are focused on attracting more businesses, creating more jobs, generating more wealth, and so forth. There is little or no attention paid to the appropriateness of the businesses attracted to the local economy or their complementarity to existing businesses; the quality of the jobs created; or the nature and distribution of the wealth created. Even those economic developers who are focused on entrepreneurship tend to pay the most attention to the number of new businesses created, the number of entrepreneurs to whom information has been handed off, or the amount of revenue these entrepreneurial ventures generate. Little thought appears to be given to measures of quality, such as the skill levels of the entrepreneurs or the effectiveness and efficiency with which they move their companies through the stages in the business life cycle (i.e., the quality and strength of their businesses).

In part, this lack of attention to quality in favor of quantity is a function of poor performance evaluation. As was noted in chapter 1, most economic development organizations are structured as publics or nonprofits. Because these organizations lack the market signals (e.g., sales, profits) enjoyed by for-profits, they are not accustomed to thinking in terms of performance outcomes. Public and nonprofit economic developers tend to keep track of outputs, which measure quantity (maintenance or growth) and are not oriented toward capturing the true impact of their efforts. They have been aided and abetted in this partial approach by the governments and philanthropic organizations that fund them, which, themselves, are not subject to market discipline. As more market-oriented practices creep into public and nonprofit operations, this is slowly but steadily changing. Nevertheless, there is a very long way yet to go.

The lack of a performance orientation, however, is not the only reason why current economic development practice errs on the side of growth over development. Growth is more readily understood. It is easier for politicians and other officials to convey to the public. It can be achieved in shorter periods of time (i.e., election cycles). Finally, it appeals to our society's immediate gratification mindset. Conversely, development requires patience because it involves a long-term process. It is complex and dynamic; therefore, it is neither easy to understand nor easy to explain to others.

The remainder of this chapter discusses the meaning of development, and why it should be given more importance in the field of economic development than it currently receives. This chapter also examines the role of development in fostering entrepreneurship and the need to both develop individual entrepreneurs and to create a framework within which to cultivate them.

WHAT IT MEANS TO DEVELOP

As suggested previously, economic development presently "talks the talk but does not walk the walk." We know why, and that is suggestive of what it will take to successfully market the concept of development. However, the question of equal or greater importance to "why?" is "how?" How do we go about putting development back into economic development?

In order to answer this question, we must first understand what *development* means and what it means to develop someone or something. *Webster's Seventh New Collegiate Dictionary* defines *develop* as "to go through a process of natural growth, differentiation, or evolution by successive change." Thus, growth is part, *but only part*, of the development process. This definition also suggests that development is systematic, following a series of progressive steps that distinguish and advance the person or thing being developed.

This further suggests that, if done well, development enhances quality. The person or thing being developed becomes better in some way(s). Development, then, produces a transformation—a leap to a higher level of performance or a deep change.[1] This cannot take place through a simple transaction, or even a series of disconnected transactions over time. It can only happen through a long-term, highly coordinated succession of intensive interactions between those being developed and those who would develop them. In other words, development must be both systematic and systemic, which is what makes it complex.

The mere fact that something is complex or difficult, however, does not grant us license to ignore or short-cut it. There is a *Tao* to development, which is disregarded only to our detriment. This is why economic developers are notorious for being faddish—chasing the latest "big thing" being hawked by the guru of the moment. There is little or no commitment to the process of true development. It is routinely argued to be unaffordable in terms of time and money. Yet, this is the lament of failed societies throughout history. The simple fact is that we cannot afford *not* to invest in our own development. This implies investment in developing individuals and in the infrastructure necessary to develop individuals. These are two different things, commonly confused. One is not sufficient without the other. We now turn to a discussion of how this line of thinking is applied to entrepreneurs and entrepreneurship.

THE IMPORTANCE OF DEVELOPING ENTREPRENEURS

If it is accepted, as we argued in chapter 1, that entrepreneurship lies at the essence of economic development, then it follows that genuinely successful economic development must focus on the development of individual entrepreneurs and their companies and the development of an infrastructure to support this effort. To date, economic developers (who pursue the facilitation of entrepreneurship as an economic development strategy) are not effectively developing individual entrepreneurs and their companies. This is true for a variety of reasons that we have discussed elsewhere.[2] However, the principle reason is that most economic developers lack the experience and level of skill necessary to truly transform the skill sets of entrepreneurs and would-be entrepreneurs—it is not their forte.[3]

What economic developers are more recently doing well is laying the groundwork and building the infrastructure for successful entrepreneurship. One only has to look at the work of organizations such as the Rural Policy Research Institute (RUPRI) Center for Rural Entrepreneurship, the Hometown Competitiveness program, and the Sirolli Institute in rural areas; and the Local Initiatives Support Corporation (LISC) and local community development corporations in urban neighborhoods to see the progress being made in this arena. These organizations, and several others like them, are teaching local leadership about entrepreneurship and its value to the economy, building alliances among local and regional organizations to support entrepreneurship, and linking sources of funding to these efforts. While this is important, and even admirable, what they don't seem to recognize is that this is not enough; half the formula for ultimate success is missing.[4]

This is the ongoing weakness of policy approaches to fostering entrepreneurship. They focus on context to the detriment of content. The underlying thinking is that we in the public and nonprofit sectors cannot really do anything about the content—we cannot actually make entrepreneurs good at what they do; that is up to them—but if we set the right context, good things will happen. This is, essentially, another manifestation of the "if we build it, they will come" attitude that has become the subject of ridicule by economic development critics.

Undoubtedly, this context-setting focus is pursued with sincerity, but it is based on two false perceptions: (1) that there exists an actual link between the context setters and the entrepreneurs, and (2) that entrepreneurs are essentially all the same, with the same needs and same skill sets. Taking these misperceptions in turn, we offer several observations.

First, we would argue that there is no real link between public and nonprofit context builders and entrepreneurs, in most cases. In some instances, it is because the entrepreneurs are unaware of these efforts on their behalf. In most cases, however, it is because public and nonprofit economic developers have no credibility with entrepreneurs, and, therefore, the latter do not trust the former. Some entrepreneurs are merely suspicious of the intentions of governments, having been hurt by onerous regulations and/or tax policies that are burdensome to small businesses. Other entrepreneurs have been disappointed by the programs offered by economic developers in which they have taken part—programs that have not helped them solve their problems. Whatever the reason, entrepreneurs typically do not participate at the level imagined by the policymakers and implementers at the time they planned their programs. This leads to frustration on the part of the economic developers, who often ascribe this low level of participation to a lack of entrepreneurs in their locales, to a nonexistent "entrepreneurial culture," or to a need for better advertising.

The reality is that public and nonprofit economic developers do not know how to connect with entrepreneurs. They are like academic theoreticians who do not understand why their conceptual models are not embraced and utilized by practitioners, when in fact these models are not actionable. Economic developers are unable to make their context-building programs truly actionable, because most of them have never been entrepreneurs and, therefore, do not really understand what it is to have "skin in the game" (e.g., waking up at night in a cold sweat wondering how you will make Friday's payroll). How can we honestly expect people who have no entrepreneurial experience to connect with entrepreneurs?

The second major misperception of economic developers is that all entrepreneurs are essentially the same. In part, this is a matter of convenience. It is easier and less expensive to adopt programs that are of a one-size-fits-all nature. However, this is also another instance of a lack of real understanding of entrepreneurs, their needs, and the variation that exists in their skill levels. If economic developers do not understand entrepreneurs or assume they are like everyone else, then how can we expect them to be of genuine help?

In fact, entrepreneurs are not all the same. They have differing needs. This is where economic developers could have a greater positive impact on entrepreneurship, if they would take the time to carefully assess their client entrepreneurs' needs and tailor their interventions accordingly. We have defined entrepreneurial needs elsewhere as obstacles to getting and using resources required for success and have offered a tool for making that crucial assessment.[5] Yet, the general reaction from economic developers has been that such an assessment is too difficult and time-consuming to undertake on a regular basis. In the interest of saving time, they apparently are willing to be irrelevant to the very entrepreneurs it is their mission to serve.[6]

Entrepreneurs are also different from each other in terms of their level of skill. This is important to recognize, because it is the mastery of a skill set that underlies success in entrepreneurship.[7] Entrepreneurs come to entrepreneurship, at any given point in time, at varying skill levels. There are nascent entrepreneurs who are starting a business for the first time. They have no experience and, therefore, few if any skills. At the other end of the spectrum are serial entrepreneurs, who have started several businesses and have succeeded with some and failed with others. They have a much higher level of skill. There are many other entrepreneurs whose skills fall somewhere between these extremes. Being able to measure entrepreneurship skills in a meaningful way and use that knowledge to target assistance appropriately is vital to developing entrepreneurs.

This brings us back to the original point about economic developers having the capability to create infrastructure for supporting entrepreneurs, but lacking the competencies necessary to *develop* entrepreneurs and their companies—creating the context but lacking the content. We have attributed much of this to a very limited understanding of entrepreneurship and entrepreneurs. This major deficiency becomes a fatal flaw, because what we are calling the "content" of true enterprise development requires the ability to transform the skill set of the entrepreneur so that, in turn, she can transform her company (i.e., grow it by changing its structure to allow it to move efficiently and effectively through the stages in the life cycle of businesses). This is what we mean by the "development" of the entrepreneur, and it is not something that just anyone can do. Only someone with previous entrepreneurship experience can understand this transformative process and help someone else through it.

Thus, because traditional public and nonprofit economic developers do not understand entrepreneurship, they are severely restricted in their ability to foster it. This is not to say that they cannot add value, but they need to stick to what they do best, which is the building and maintenance of the infrastructure that supports entrepreneurship. Furthermore, they should embrace something that entrepreneurs have long understood—the value of building an entrepreneurial team. Successful entrepreneurs know that they do not possess all of the skills required to launch and grow an enterprise. Therefore, they assemble a team of individuals that has the complementary skill sets to pursue the economic opportunity around which the venture is built. Good entrepreneurs know what they know and what they don't know.[8] Likewise, successful economic developers will recognize their limitations and seek out partners who possess the expertise they lack. That is, they will pursue entrepreneurs to lead the effort to develop entrepreneurs and their companies.

THE FRAMEWORK FOR DEVELOPING ENTREPRENEURS

Because it is transformative, the process of developing entrepreneurs is complex. It is not something that one just leaps into and muddles through, even if one has previous experience as an entrepreneur. It requires a set of lenses or a framework that can be used to organize the complexity so that it can be managed and acted upon.

In the following three chapters, we incrementally lay out such a framework. We call this framework the Pipeline of Entrepreneurs and Enterprises. We begin our explication of the Pipeline with a discussion of the skills required for successful entrepreneurship.

3

The Skill Ladder

The reasonable man adapts himself to the world, the unreasonable man adapts the world to himself, therefore, all progress depends on the unreasonable man.

—George Bernard Shaw

In this chapter, we examine the first key variable in the Pipeline of Entrepreneurs and Enterprises—skills. Figure 3.1 illustrates our thinking regarding the differences in skill levels among entrepreneurs. The ladder depicts the idea that skill development is an upward progression. We will explain this idea more fully as this chapter unfolds.

One formative experience that led to our discovery of skill level differences was a series of evaluations we received after delivering a training program to more than 600 economic developers, businesspeople, and policymakers. Half the participants ranked the program as the best they had ever participated in. We were very gratified by their responses and comments. The other half rated the program as the worst they had ever participated in on this subject. No one was in-between. For several years, we mulled over these results and wondered: were we all in the same room, participating in the same training? How could that be? What could explain why the responses were so extreme?

Then it dawned on us: to use the language of skill levels that we will be introducing shortly—if we had "pitched" the program to the Single A (labeled A on the figure) level of understanding, the material would appear to be over the heads of the Rookies who are lower on the skill ladder, and beneath the ability of the Double As (AA on the figure), who are higher. Anyone in the training sessions that was not a Single A would find the program inappropriate to their needs!

FIGURE 3.1.
The Skill Ladder

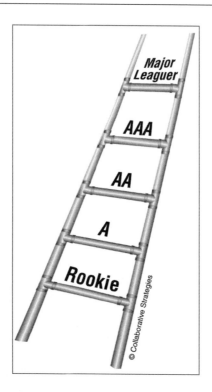

Well, from the point of view of efficiency and effectiveness, a 50 percent ceiling to our hit rate was completely unacceptable to us. One has to make some choice about a level to which to pitch any program. But who wants to walk into a room to deliver a program or a service where the absolute best one could do is 50 percent, no matter how hard or skillfully one tried? We would rather have the opportunity to hit 100 percent, however unrealistic that might prove to be in practice.

Not long afterwards, we were talking to a group of Chamber of Commerce executives from West Michigan about the Pipeline, in regard to a series of CEO forums they were running with mixed success. After a very short conversation, it became clear to us that the CEO groups that were successful were working because by *accident*, a critical mass of participants was at the same skill level, had similar needs, and could easily form bonds of trust. In the same way, those that were unsuccessful were not working because by *accident*, the participants were all at different skill levels. The Chamber execs agreed with our diagnosis; it helped them make sense of the divergent results as well as their own personal knowledge of the individual participants involved.

We stress the word by "accident" because the Chamber management had no way to distinguish in advance between the skill levels of the various participants in their program and to make decisions on that basis. Who would want to operate by accident, when they could be more effective operating on purpose? But to be more intentional would require that we know our clients' skill level up front and then be able to match our offering to it. Out of this need grew our intense desire to understand and assess skill level differences in entrepreneurs.

DEFINING AN ENTREPRENEUR

A story that a fellow speaker at an economic development conference[1] told about his grandfather epitomizes for us the definition of an entrepreneur: When a certain soldier, who fought for the South, returned home to the devastation wrought by the Civil War, he joined the community of starving survivors discussing their plight. He quickly tired of the incessant complaints and unending conversation and left. He went into the woods, cut down timber, used some of the logs to build a raft, floated the raft and logs 20 miles down the river to the nearest town, and sold the timber in order to buy a donkey. He rode back home, gave the donkey to his neighbor in exchange for the neighbor's promise to use the donkey to plow the soldier's fields as well as his own, and then went into the woods to harvest more timber. He repeated this activity until he had built a successful timber business and helped reestablish his community's economy.

Entrepreneurs are individuals who create value or wealth (i.e., business assets) by identifying and capturing market opportunities. They are the "engines" of economic development in a community. This story raises a simple question: what was different about this individual? This opportunity, to go into the woods and harvest timber, was open to everyone in his community; why was he the only one that did something about it? To us, the difference lies in what this soldier saw and did, not what or who he was. He envisioned a possibility that did not yet exist in reality—and by taking action brought that possibility into being. Successfully engaging in this behavior requires certain skills.

THREE KEY BELIEFS ABOUT ENTREPRENEURSHIP

Our conception of entrepreneurship is built on three key beliefs:

1. Entrepreneurs are successful to the extent that they have the necessary skills.
2. Entrepreneurs come to entrepreneurship at different levels of skill.
3. Entrepreneurial skills can be developed.

Successful Entrepreneurs Have Skills

Over the years, we have worked with the owners of many different kinds of businesses, representing different industries, markets, products and services, sizes in terms of sales, and levels of technological sophistication. We observed that their business success rarely had to do with their technical skills alone (many of the less successful firms were led by entrepreneurs who had better technical skills), nor their choice of industry or market, although those things are not unimportant. We found successful entrepreneurs in market segments that the business press or conventional business wisdom would say could never support a profitable business. We found unsuccessful entrepreneurs in sectors that were supposedly sure-fire bets. No matter what the industry, the distinguishing feature in their success was the owner's entrepreneurial skills: that is, their ability to identify and capture a market opportunity.

What do we mean by skills? *We define skill as the ability to perform a particular action or task on a consistent basis, at a high level of performance, without a great deal of conscious thinking or attention, to achieve a desired outcome.* A skill is something that would enable one to produce a particular behavior or even a range of behaviors. But a skill cannot be simply reduced to a behavior; a specific behavior that is "entrepreneurial" in one context will not necessarily be so in another time and space.

Skills are also not competencies. In business literature, the term *competency* usually denotes a broad category of knowledge, like *communication* or *organization*. At such a high level of abstraction, competencies do not and cannot indicate specifically what to do, how to do it, and under what circumstances—the details that define practical or applied knowledge. By contrast, when we refer to skills, we are talking about something that is actionable and reproducible or repeatable.

Entrepreneurs Have Different Levels of Skill

It seems obvious that entrepreneurs have different degrees of skills. We easily recognize differences in levels of skill in every field of human activity. When explaining differences in skill levels to those unfamiliar with business, one colleague of ours asks if they can tell whether the basketball players they see when they turn on the television are college or professional. They recognize the differences immediately, without having to give it any thought. When thinking about entrepreneurship, we rarely ask ourselves what is the source of these differences in skill.

Entrepreneurial Skills Can Be Developed

In our experience, most people believe that differences in ability are innate—due to personal traits or characteristics, about which nothing can be done. Essentially, they argue that entrepreneurs are born and not made. This position persists despite the fact that there is no research to support it. In fact, the search for the inborn personality traits of entrepreneurs has been a favorite research topic of academics, as demonstrated by the large number of studies that have addressed this question.[2] However, after 60 years, no one has yet established a correlation (let alone proven a causal relationship) between any personality traits and entrepreneurial behavior.

The most devastating aspect of this position doesn't lie in its truth or falsity (about which humans will debate until the end of time), but rather in its implications for practice. Many people complain that there are no (or few) entrepreneurs in their community, and that may be true. But the question becomes what, if anything, can we do about it? Those that believe entrepreneurial ability is due to inborn characteristics are in essence saying that there is *nothing* that can be done. We can only seek out and support the ones who are born with the "right stuff" whenever they come along. If, as economic developers, we take this position seriously, there is really nothing to be done at work each day, short of referring the parents in our communities to genetic engineers.

But if entrepreneurs are made and not born, as we believe,[3] then this position on innate traits is an abdication of the responsibility for developing entrepreneurs. As Kegan and Lahey have noted, "Leaders who seek to win a war for talent by conceiving of capability as a fixed resource to be found 'out there' put themselves and their organizations at a serious disadvantage. In contrast, leaders who ask themselves, 'What can I do to make my setting the most fertile ground in the world for the growth of talent?' put themselves in the best position to succeed."[4]

FARM SYSTEMS FOR DEVELOPING SKILLS

During our investigation into how skills are developed, we were inspired by what is perhaps the largest and most systematic arrangement in the world for developing skills, the farm system of sports. In the United States, baseball's farm system is the oldest and most established, but such systems exist in all sports: football, basketball, hockey, and others. Around the world, the best example would be for the game of soccer.

We were also influenced by the journey of jazz artists in the 1930s, as they left the rural south for St. Louis, for example, where they waited until after midnight to sit in with the house band, after the customers had left. Once they had earned their "chops," they were asked to play with the band in front of the paying customers. These musicians started in the smallest clubs with the least reputation and repeated the process until they climbed to the upper echelon in that city's music scene. Then they moved from there to Chicago, and maybe on to New York City, known as the Big Apple, so-called because gigs there generated the most "sugar" or money. Whether so labeled or not, a farm system existed for jazz musicians during that period, and one of the complaints of jazz musicians today is about the decay of that infrastructure and the loss of opportunity it implies for young artists.

As we looked elsewhere, we began to notice that farm systems of this nature, and the skill-level rankings they are based on, are ubiquitous: they can be found in the arts, horseracing, auto racing, chess, bridge, and the military, as well as in other fields of music—literally every field of endeavor in which mastery is required. A recent *New York Times* article even notes that "A baseball-like farm system has developed in American opera in recent decades, as more and more young-artist programs have sprouted up around the country."[5] In fact, opera houses around the United States are ranked by members of the profession, and a singer's success is clearly a function of the level of opera house in which he or she has performed.

What these systems show us is that a hierarchy of skill and performance exists. No one moves from novice to master in a single step—there are no overnight successes—they develop in discrete and manageable chunks (i.e., rungs on the ladder). While the extremes of novice and expert are beginning to be recognized in the field of entrepreneurship, our contribution is to differentiate entrepreneurial skill by specific levels and to define or operationalize these differences.

INTRODUCING SKILL LEVELS

There are four dimensions that define the level of skill at which an entrepreneur functions:[6]

- Technical skills—the ability to perform the key operations of that business
- Managerial skills—the ability to organize and efficiently manage the operations
- Entrepreneurial skills—the ability to identify market opportunities and create solutions that capture those opportunities
- Personal maturity—self-awareness, willingness and ability to accept responsibility, emotional development, and creative ability.

These dimensions form a pattern of five distinct skill levels, as described in Table 3.1.

TABLE 3.1.
The Ladder of Entrepreneurial Skills

Skill Level	Techinical Skills	Managerial Skills	Entrepreneurial Skills	Personal Maturity
Major Leaguer	Outstanding	Outstanding	Outstanding	Outstanding
AAA	High	High	High	High
AA	High	Medium	Medium	Medium
A	Medium / High	Low	Low	Low
Rookie	Low / Medium	No / Low	No / Low	No / Low

Adapted from Gregg A. Lichtenstein and T. S. Lyons, "The Entrepreneurial Development System: Transforming Business Talent and Community Economies," *Economic Development Quarterly* 15, no. 1 (2001): 3–20. © Collaborative Strategies, LLC.

Rookies, as the label suggests, come to entrepreneurship with few if any business skills. Sometimes they may have a reasonable degree of technical skills in their chosen field, whether it is machine tool building, operating clinical trials for pharmaceutical companies, or specialized materials recycling, but frequently their managerial and entrepreneurial skills are missing. Their businesses tend to run them.[7]

These individuals might have been thrust into entrepreneurship due to circumstances such as a layoff, or, as is more typical, they saw another entrepreneur doing something and thought: if that person can be successful, why can't I? But they did not realize that the actual work itself is just a small part of what it takes to operate a business.

Stronger managerial and entrepreneurial skills begin to appear among those in the Single A level, which enable entrepreneurs at this level to operate businesses that are small in size and fairly simple in scope.

Double As have more highly developed business skills, which are a result of either having worked in a number of existing companies or having started other businesses.

Triple As (AAA in the figure) are experienced, serial entrepreneurs with a great deal of sophistication. They usually launch ventures with high-risk, high-reward profiles that are highly innovative, either in terms of the offering or their business model.

Major Leaguers are highly successful, seasoned entrepreneurs who are usually involved in ventures whose goal is to create entirely new markets based on major market shifts or scientific discoveries.

Through our work in the field, we have learned that there is a level below the Rookies, which would need to be addressed in any systemic effort to develop entrepreneurs, particularly in developing countries. Individuals at this level are simply not ready to be in business. This level may include youth entrepreneurs, individuals in welfare-to-work programs, and certain kinds of participants in the underground economy. We believe that they are candidates for formal and informal learning opportunities as well as apprenticeships, but they clearly require additional preparation before they should engage in the risk of starting and owning their own business. (For a more detailed discussion of this subject, see Scenario 11 in Chapter 8 on page 153.)

OBSERVATIONS ABOUT SKILL LEVELS

Before we present deeper descriptions of the differences in skill levels, a few observations are in order.

Entrepreneurs at each skill level think as well as behave very differently from those at other levels. As will become clear in the upcoming examples, their mindsets vary in terms of their conception of their business, the timeframe in which they operate, their ability to delegate, their span of control, their ability to abstract from concrete reality, the scope of their experiences, and the way they categorize them.

Each higher skill level represents a greater ability than the skill levels below it. It is not that the more skilled entrepreneurs are smarter; it is that they possess a different (both broader and deeper) capacity to deal with uncertainty, risk, the future, leverage, and innovation.

Everyone must pass through the lower levels to get to the higher levels of skill. In other words, according to our terminology, everyone starts as a Rookie, and there are no such things as overnight successes in the development of entrepreneurial skills (nor, others would argue, in the development of any other sophisticated skill). Those entrepreneurs that we admire as stars today were, at the beginning of their careers, as naive, unskilled, and indistinguishable as any other new businessperson.

Individuals can be (entrepreneurial) Rookies despite their level of technical skills. We know many brilliant individuals with technical Ph.D.s who have never met a payroll, risked a dime, dealt with high levels of uncertainty, or put together a profit-and-loss statement, and for whom those skills, while learnable, were not, at that point in time, easy to perform. Their high level of performance in one field does not automatically, nor necessarily, transfer over to another (even though, as those of us who have worked extensively with scientists and Ph.D. level researchers can attest, they often believe that it does). This behavior is also exhibited by some professionals like doctors and lawyers who invest in businesses.

As is true in every field of expertise, the distribution of skills tends to be a pyramid—very broad at the bottom (with lots of individuals at the lower levels) and narrow at the top. This pattern is to be expected, given the nature of expertise or skill mastery and what it takes to develop in terms of motivation, discipline, and time. For example, an estimated 2 million to 3.7 million kids in the United States play baseball annually, but only 1,200 make it to the Major Leagues.[8] For every general or admiral of the highest rank in the four branches of the armed forces, there are approximately 6,473 officers and 33,700 enlisted men.[9] Individual entrepreneurs at the Triple A skill level are very rare; enterprises frequently achieve that skill level only by forming a team with complementary capabilities. As we continue to assess entrepreneurial skills, we will learn more about the shape of the distribution curve and the factors in a particular population that influence it.

The patterns described in Table 3.1 are generalizations. It is unusual across the various dimensions on which we assess skill levels for someone to uniformly be rated at the same level. It is much more likely that an entrepreneur is assessed at different skill levels on different dimensions. For example, an entrepreneur might be a Double A in terms of her entrepreneurial skills and a Rookie in terms of her management skills. Her rating across these two dimensions might average out to place her as a Single A. As a result, entrepreneurs tend to possess a unique profile representing a distinctive combination, particularly at the higher skill levels. Our assignment of them to a single skill level captures their central tendency.

As noted previously, individual entrepreneurs operating at the Triple A or Major League skill levels are very rare; it is more likely that those skill levels are achieved by a team made up of individuals with complementary capabilities who work well together. Many highly touted entrepreneurs are really members of either partnerships or teams, without which they would have been unable to achieve such high levels of success. Well-known examples include Walt and Roy Disney, Bill Gates and Paul Allen or Steve Ballmer, and Steve Jobs and Steve Wozniak. In a simplification of the division of labor, typically one individual is the face of the company and the other functions as the inside man; the former the visionary and dreamer, and the latter the detail person that implements those visions.

The management skills required in an entrepreneurial enterprise are of a completely different nature from those required to manage a stable, existing business. We are not talking about the skills involved in running a $20 million venture, with its accounting, human resource, and information systems already in place, when the leadership position is assumed at $19 million in revenue. We are talking about the management skills required to build the organization while simultaneously generating revenue; that is, literally laying down the railroad tracks just slightly in advance of the oncoming train. This is the management challenge that occurs when a business is growing from $0 in sales to $500,000, from $1 to $5 million, or from $10 to $25 million. Each new level in growth requires a complete restructuring of the business, entirely new operating systems, and an accompanying increase in skill. All the while, one must keep the revenue-generating machine going; in other words, there is no stopping the train while laying the tracks.

The dimension of personal maturity (also known as emotional intelligence)[10] is usually an indication of how likely it is that someone will be able and willing to perform the work necessary to move up to a higher skill level.[11]

Interacting and working with entrepreneurs at the various skill levels is quite different. One does not interact with Rookies in the same way one does with Double As, just as one does not coach grade school students in sports the same as one would college athletes. As a result, someone who can coach or consult effectively at one skill level will not necessarily be effective at another. It is not a question of content knowledge; it is a reflection of the ability to connect and transmit that knowledge to others. And as in all things, rare is the individual who can coach absolutely anyone. Most of us mere mortals naturally tend to specialize. As we will discuss later, this obvious but simple truth is often overlooked in the design of technical assistance and entrepreneurship education programs.

WHAT ARE THE DIFFERENCES IN SKILL LEVELS?

One of the ways to explain the differences in the behavior of entrepreneurs at the various skill levels is to examine how each one conceives of their business and their role in it. People who advise entrepreneurs often talk about the need for them to work on their business, rather than in it, but what this means in terms of content differs at each skill level. We will see what these distinctions reveal about the thinking behind the entrepreneur's behavior.

Rookies

Rookies, for example, conceive of their business as work: a set of activities that they are responsible for performing. When you ask a Rookie how their business is doing, they will tell you whether they are busy or not. They will never tell you about their sales revenue (a Single A concern), nor whether or not they are making a profit (a Double A response). Their assumption is that if they are busy, they must be making money.

We understand that to some people, this may sound like a caricature or a criticism. It is not meant to be and should not be viewed in that way. We are simply describing how entrepreneurs at this level, almost categorically, think about their business and their role in it. Rookies are the "doers" in their business, and most of them do not believe that they are adding value unless they are actually doing the work. As you can imagine, this way of thinking will prevent them from successfully growing their business to any significant size, because unless they change, their output will be limited by their ability to do the work.

We have found that this particular conceptualization of the business exists for all Rookie entrepreneurs regardless of their age, gender, background, educational level, or technical sophistication. At this skill level, this is the way they conceive and make sense of their world. Rookies believe that if they work hard, they will succeed—that hard work is both necessary and sufficient to achieve success. All of the other keys to business success are basically not part of their thinking.

Rookies are usually immersed in their work, and for that reason it tends to control them. Rarely do Rookies know if they are working on the "right" things. That question is beyond them—it is hidden from their view. If they are lucky, they can earn enough from their business to survive, meaning to keep working, but rarely enough for them to thrive and get ahead financially. For Rookies, working "in" their business *is* the same thing as working "on" their business.

Single A

Movement to the Single A level represents a shift in thinking—and this is a critical feature of the passage from any skill level to another. What was once in the background, hidden from view, shifts to the foreground and becomes something to which the entrepreneur can now attend. For the Single A, working on the business, rather than in it, means taking control of the work, and in that light, for example, questioning whether one is working on the right things. To answer that, one must understand the goal of one's efforts. For Single As, that goal is income—for the business and for themselves.

Where Rookies own their "work," Single As own a "job." The extent to which they learn to control the work means that they can gain control over the income that job generates. Where Rookies perform work "in" a job, Single As perform a job, in their business. If successful, they will generate a stream of income sufficient to meet their needs and more. Their goal is to become income rich. Their business is their job (rather than their work, as in the case of Rookies), and its value is measured by how much income (direct as well as indirect compensation in the form of benefits) it generates for them. Single As identify themselves with the job, which, while it represents an advancement over the thinking of a Rookie entrepreneur, can in turn represent a limitation in moving to the next skill level.

Double A

Whereas Single As own a job, Double As own and control a business. The goal of entrepreneurs at this level is twofold: (1) to build an asset that generates revenue with or without the owner having to have a job, and (2) to build an asset that has market value—meaning it can be sold at a profitable price, with a sizeable return on the entrepreneur's investment of time and resources. For a Double A, the job becomes a means to these ends. The goal is to increase the value of the asset. This is the sense in which Double As are working on the business rather than in it.

Triple A

Whereas the Double A owns a business, the Triple A owns and controls a portfolio of business assets. What this means specifically is that Triple As conceive of their business as a system of related or interlocking assets. For example, the Double A owner of a construction company will buy a crane in order to complete a project and view it as an expense that will hopefully be paid for by the project revenue. The Triple A owner of a construction company buys the crane but views it instead as an asset and the project revenue as the down payment or installment on that asset, which can now be used to generate a new stream of revenue from other projects. If the acquisition of assets is synergistic, then an investment in one asset will not only yield income by itself, but it will help when combined with other assets to generate more revenue than the sum of the revenue of the parts (this is leverage). The goal of the Triple A is to generate multiple, but synergistic revenue streams that increases the value of her portfolio of assets.

Major League

Major league entrepreneurs, by contrast, own and control an innovation system (a system of business portfolios). They are focused on creating and managing a brand or institution that will leave a long-term legacy.

Entrepreneurs at this level are designers and orchestrators of systems of businesses (each of which is a portfolio of assets). Bill Gates, Steve Jobs, and Michael Dell are well-known examples.[12]

This differentiation by level applies to other dimensions or aspects of the skills necessary to be a successful entrepreneur. While neither time nor space permit us to present a fully detailed representation of the functioning at each skill level, we would like to offer several additional examples.

DASHBOARD METAPHOR

One thing that characterizes entrepreneurs at different skill levels is the number of variables they are able to attend to at one time. Using a car's dashboard as a metaphor for financial monitoring, Rookies only pay attention to one gauge—and it will be whatever gauge happens to be of most interest to them (notice that we said interest, not importance). If they like speed, it will be their speedometer (i.e., how fast sales are coming in). If they are concerned with resources, they will monitor the amount in their gas tank (i.e., the dollars that remain in their bank account). But the attention they give to this matter is single-minded (they are only able to see one thing at a time) and subjective.

Single As pay attention to a number of gauges on their dashboard, but each gauge is seen separately, that is, in isolation from one another. It is only at the Double A level that the entrepreneur fully understands that there is a relationship among these gauges and the operations of the car that they represent.

How does this metaphor reflect differences in financial management skills? Rookies do not engage in financial management, or if they do, they only perform it in the most limited sense. We have often asked Rookies how they know if they are doing well in their business. One said, in all seriousness, that if there is still money in his checking account at the end of the month after he has paid his bills, then he must be doing all right. Another said that if the chair he is sitting on is still there and hasn't been taken away yet, he is still around to work another day and he must be doing okay.[13]

To move to the Single A skill level in terms of financial management, Rookies must learn to prepare income statements and begin to use them to manage their business. At the Single A level, entrepreneurs are now paying attention to at least two gauges—revenue and expenses—but their challenge, and the skill that will enable them to become Double As, is to understand the relationship of those two gauges to each other and how that relationship produces either profits or losses.

TIMEFRAME DIFFERENCES

Entrepreneurs at the various skill levels also differ in terms of the timeframes at which they can operate. Rookies have a timeframe of 3 to 90 days. This is not to say that they can't dream of events or circumstances that take place much further into the future. This timeframe describes the limits of their ability to plan and manage the work that they need to perform in order to bring those dreams about. Now each entrepreneur may have a different reason why this timeframe is a limitation for them, which is why the process of helping someone overcome this limitation must be customized to their particular need, but this limitation will be the same for all Rookies. As a result, Rookies will not be able to produce a real annual budget based on realistic operating estimates until they can overcome whatever obstacle holds them back from operating with a longer timeframe.

Double As, for example, have a timeframe of one to two years. That is why you will observe them regularly engaging in projects that fall within that time duration, such as workflow reengineering, new product development (consisting of minor modifications to offerings that already exist in the world), and leadership development programs.

WORKFLOW PERCEPTIONS

In terms of operations and workflow, one of the behaviors that characterizes an entrepreneur who is moving from the Rookie to the Single A level is control over the work by organizing it according to functions (even if he or she is still performing all of the functions themselves). This movement to functional specialization enables a significant increase in efficiency and performance, and, if done right, translates directly to increases in the top and the bottom line of the business.

However, as we all know, at some point in the growth of a business, functional specialization can turn into silo behavior, in which the separate parts of the business make decisions in their own individual interest at the expense of the business as a whole. Consistent with the piecemeal way in which Single As compartmentalize the financial gauges in their business, the marketing department focuses on generating sales revenue irrespective of the cost to produce the offering, while manufacturing focuses on minimizing the expenses in producing the offering, irrespective of the revenue that they generate. This behavior, which is rational from each function's particular point of view, places them at odds with one another and creates a conflict in the business.

To overcome this limitation, Double A-thinking is required. A Double A entrepreneur redesigns the incentives in her business so that the parts now look at their contribution to the whole rather than just to their department. One of the ways in which this can be achieved is to measure the performance of both marketing and operations in terms of the profitability of their results (the relationship between revenue and expenses).

A PATTERN OF INCREASING CAPABILITIES

As we examine how entrepreneurs at each skill level both think and behave, we observe a pattern of increasing scope, complexity, and capability. At each higher skill level in an entrepreneur's development, what had previously controlled the entrepreneur (meaning what was beyond their control) now becomes an object of their attention and control. Each higher level includes what existed at the lower skill level but introduces a fundamentally new capability that transcends and reorganizes the way in which the lower level operated. This higher-order skill represents a significant change in thinking and behavior, not a marginal or incremental improvement. It marks a vertical shift in skill development.

Another example that helps make this progression of capability clear has to do with how the role of management changes at each skill level. At the Rookie level, the challenge is for entrepreneurs to learn how to manage "themselves." Single As must learn how to manage "others." Double As must learn how to manage managers (who in turn manage others), and Triple As must learn how to manage entrepreneurs. Each higher level increases and expands the entrepreneur's capabilities but at the same time includes all of the capabilities below it.

We are not just speaking loosely or conceptually here. There is a real difference between skills and abstract knowledge. To operate at a higher skill level, an entrepreneur must be able to walk the walk, not just talk the talk. We have met many M.B.A.s who sound like Double As because they know the language and throw around the right terms. But when you scratch below the surface, explore what they do rather than what they say, you find that if they lack the skills, the concepts they use are empty of any experience, and, as a result, of any meaning or power. This is not only true of highly credentialed individuals, but of others, who think that what they have read in books is sufficient to give them the ability to execute those ideas. In order to see these differences in capability more clearly, let's look at how entrepreneurs at different skill levels solve the same problem.

SOLVING A PROBLEM AT DIFFERENT SKILL LEVELS

Entrepreneurs at different skill levels will solve the same problem very differently. Because innovative solutions are the hallmark of entrepreneurs, let's examine an example of how a technical problem would be solved by individuals at different skill levels. This example, drawn from a paper written by Boris Zlotin and Alla Zusman of Ideation International,[14] describes the results of a project whose goal is to reduce the vibration of an electrical generator being utilized in a transport situation. Table 3.2 describes the solutions that were developed at different levels of thinking. Note that we have reversed the way we normally list the skills, to start with the lowest level first.

This example suggests that there are levels to innovations, and that an entrepreneur's ability to conceive of and implement an innovation or market opportunity will depend on their skill level. This means that if a situation demands a more sophisticated, complex innovation, we will need entrepreneurs with higher skills in order to generate and implement them. This also suggests that market opportunities are not things that objectively exist out there in the world but are rather subjectively defined by the entrepreneur. If this is so, then the nature of the market opportunity that an entrepreneur will perceive will very much depend on his or her skill level.

This perspective presents a significant challenge to the best practices approach to business. That approach argues that there is a single best practice that exists for a business, subject of course to differences in competitive strategy and business model selected. However, our framework suggests that what is defined as best practice will also be heavily influenced by the skill level of the entrepreneur.

For example, lean manufacturing, where appropriate, is a best practice not only for manufacturing but for other operations as well. It removes inefficiencies, reduces inventory, and increases productivity by

TABLE 3.2.
Technical Innovation by Skill Level

Level of Skill/ Thinking Required	Technical Innovation or Solution	Limitation
Rookie	Install generator on rubber pads to absorb vibration. Note: this is a noninventive solution.	Vibration at certain frequencies not effectively addressed.
A	Use multilayer pads of different materials, with the thickness of each layer calculated to better reduce vibration in the given range.	Does not address haphazard impacts.
AA	Introduce pneumatic cylinders with feedback-based control mechanisms to adjust cylinder pressure according to the magnitude and direction of haphazard impacts.	Space around generator is limited; solution is expensive.
AAA	Position the generator on strong permanent magnets with electro-magnetic windings. Winding current can be changed to dampen vibration.	System has high inertia; strong electromagnetic field dissipation
Major Leaguer	Replace generator with a device that can generate electrical energy without rotating parts, which cause vibration (for example, by using isotopic elements). At the time of the project, this was an entirely new direction based on a recent scientific discovery.	System is too new; costly research and testing required.

Adapted from Boris Zlotin and Alla Zusman, *Levels of Invention and Intellectual Property Strategies* (Southfield, MI: Ideation International, 2003).

reducing manpower needs, among other outcomes. Yet, as we have observed in the preceding discussion, it requires the skills of a Double A to think in these terms and to effectively act on them.

To prematurely push an entrepreneur to adopt a business practice who is not ready, willing, and able to implement it will never be successful. We believe that this mismatch between business practice and skill level helps explain why many consulting engagements are unsuccessful. If we accept for the sake of argument that the consultants' analysis and recommendations are spot on, why are so few implemented? Developmentally, the client simply may not have been ready. For this reason, we must consider the possibility that "best" business practices will differ by skill level.

This means that a given task is not the same at each skill level. In the previous example of management, the task of management is different at each level. For a Rookie the task is to learn how to manage one's self. If a Rookie entrepreneur cannot do that, there is no way they will be capable of the Single A's management task, which is to manage others, and on up the ladder. Mastery then, is not a matter of performing the same tasks better at each higher skill level, but in fact performing very different kinds of tasks.

HOW DID WE DEVELOP THESE LEVELS?

At this point, many readers might be wondering how we arrived at these skill levels. As we mentioned in the Introduction, these findings are the result of over 25 years of work with close to 1,500 different entrepreneurs representing businesses of all kinds.

At the very beginning of this journey, we drew lines in the sand on the basis of what we knew then and made our judgments impressionistically, knowing that with a great deal of effort, we could improve them over time. We involved a number of people in the process of making these early judgments in order to offer as many different perspectives as possible. We further checked our decisions by observing entrepreneurs interacting with other entrepreneurs. Early on, we found that if two entrepreneurs in a conversation were participating equally, then it was very likely that they were both at the same skill level. If their conversation was dominated by one or the other, it was very likely that they were at different skill levels (accounting for the possibility of personality characteristics). This gave us another way to verify our judgments.

We continued to refine our judgments about the distinctions between skill levels. We developed a formal assessment tool that is administered by an experienced entrepreneur on a face-to-face basis that brought even more consistency to the process. Then we began to record the assessment interviews and transcribe them verbatim in order to distill the thinking and behaviors even further. During the process, we gained greater precision about the very language used by entrepreneurs at each of the skill levels. This led to major leaps in the quality of our assessment tool, which is currently in its third generation, having been used with more than 350 entrepreneurs in a wide variety of industries and circumstances. The transcriptions also allowed us to have other individuals review and assess those same entrepreneurs. We discovered that our tool demonstrates a high degree of inter-rater reliability (i.e., different individuals tend to arrive at similar ratings, in this case using the same tool).

Slightly more than half of these entrepreneurs participated in the coaching practice we operate—the Entrepreneurial League System®.[15] That gave us a unique vantage point (i.e., a long-term, in-depth relationship) from which to observe whether or not our original assessments of their skill levels were correct, and also what changes these entrepreneurs needed to make over time in order to substantially grow their businesses as well as move up to the next skill.

To date, we have done a great deal of work to operationalize the differences among skill levels. We have also clearly determined the specific requirements in terms of thinking and behavior that must be in place before an entrepreneur can move to the next skill level.

ARE THESE DIFFERENCES IN SKILL LEVELS REAL?

In order to answer this question, we examine data drawn from:

- Two large-scale, regional coaching programs that we operate
- A comparative analysis of entrepreneurial ophthalmologists
- An analysis of productivity of various innovations in the mining industry
- The voice of the entrepreneurs who have been exposed to the Skill Ladder

Differences in Economic Performance by Skill Level

In 2004, we implemented a large-scale regional coaching program based on the skill levels described here, called the Entrepreneurial League System®, with $2.35 million in funding from the Claude Worthington Benedum and the W. K. Kellogg Foundations.[16] The project was located in Advantage Valley—a multistate region consisting of eight counties in West Virginia (centered on the cities of Charleston and Huntington), three in eastern Kentucky, and one in southern Ohio. Over 73 entrepreneurs received coaching for a minimum of six months, during the four years the program was in operation. All were evaluated for their skill level before being placed with a coach.

In 2006, we implemented a second Entrepreneurial League System® in Central Louisiana, with $2.2 million in multiyear funding from The Rapides Foundation, a regional health care foundation created from the sale of a local hospital system.[17] Their interest in entrepreneurship was driven by the fact that health outcomes strongly correlate to average income levels in the community. If entrepreneurs could be helped to grow their businesses, create more wealth, and pay higher wages and salaries, then health outcomes would improve.

As a part of the Social Agreement® that all clients sign before they enter the Entrepreneurial League System®, entrepreneurs agree to submit quarterly data on their sales revenue, employees, percent of sales outside the region, and percent of sales outside the United States. In turn, we agree to maintain the confidentiality of this data and the anonymity of the clients by only reporting the information on an aggregate basis.

Using data submitted from clients in these two coaching programs, we have analyzed the relationship between skill level and sales revenue in order to examine the impact of skills on performance. Table 3.3 reports on the analysis of 73 clients in the Advantage Valley Entrepreneurial

TABLE 3.3.
Sales Revenue by Skill Level for Clients Participating in the Advantage Valley Entrepreneurial League System® ($N = 73$)

Skill Level (n)	Average Sales Revenue	Ratio Between Levels	Median Sales Revenue	Ratio Between Levels
AAA (0)	n/a	n/a	n/a	n/a
AA (5)	$1,480,397	1.6	$1,780,267	6.5
A (47)	$951,188	6	$273,604	10.7
Rookie (21)	$158,926	1	$25,645	1

Note: n/a expresses the fact that there were no Triple A clients in this system at the time. © Collaborative Strategies, LLC.

TABLE 3.4.

Sales Revenue by Skill Level for Clients Participating in the Entrepreneurial League System® of Central Louisiana (*N* = 109)

Skill Level (*n*)	Average Sales Revenue	Ratio Between Levels	Median Sales Revenue	Ratio Between Levels
AAA (0)	n/a	n/a	n/a	n/a
AA (13)	$5,114,762	4.9	$3,616,748	7.14
A (43)	$1,042,913	2.3	$506,375	2.1
Rookie (53)	$456,745	1	$242,665	1

Note: n/a expresses the fact that there were no Triple A clients in this system at the time. © Collaborative Strategies, LLC.

League System®. Table 3.4 examines the data from 109 clients in the Entrepreneurial League System® of Central Louisiana.

Both tables demonstrate significant differences in average sales revenue among skill levels. In Advantage Valley, the differences between Rookies and Single As are more marked, with Single As generating six times more revenue than the Rookies. In Central Louisiana, Single As generate 2.3 times more revenue than Rookies. In Advantage Valley, the Double As generate 60 percent more in revenue than the Single As. In Central Louisiana, they generate 4.9 times more revenue than the Single As.

The differences in ratios between median sales revenues among skill levels are also significant. In the Advantage Valley Entrepreneurial League System®, the median revenue figure for Double A entrepreneurs was 6.5 times higher than the median for Single A entrepreneurs. The median sales revenue for Single A entrepreneurs was 10.7 times greater than the median figure for Rookies. In the Entrepreneurial League System® of Central Louisiana, the median sales revenue for Double A entrepreneurs was 7.14 times higher than the figure for Single A entrepreneurs. The median sales figure for Single A entrepreneurs was 2.1 times higher than for the Rookies.

Another fascinating study by William Torbert, a management scientist,[18] analyzed the development levels and associated business revenues of 13 entrepreneurs. While the dataset is small, what makes this study so unusual is that all of the participants were educated as ophthalmologists and are operating their own practices in that field. This means that the analysis can isolate the impact of skill levels by holding the entrepreneurs' backgrounds and the type of business (industry, market, offering) constant. Torbert's development levels, which he refers to as Technicians, Achievers, and Strategists, closely parallel our Rookie, Single A, and Double A skill levels. Table 3.5 is adapted from his analysis.[19]

Torbert reports that annual revenues show no consistent relationship to age or the number of years that these physicians have been operating their practices. However, there are very dramatic differences by development or skill level. As in the performance analysis of the entrepreneurs in Central Louisiana and West Virginia, the average revenue is more than *three* times as large as the average for businesses at the prior level. In addition, Torbert reports that there is no overlap between sizes of practices at the different stages: the smallest practice at each level is more than twice as large as the largest practice at the prior level.

Furthermore, in terms of productivity, Torbert reports that Rookies (our terminology), "insisting on hands-on participation in every technical phase of their operations—are able to see essentially one patient at a time." Single As "delegating significant aspects of the operation to their

TABLE 3.5.
A Comparison of the Developmental/Skill Level and Annual Revenues for 13 Entrepreneurial Professional Ophthalmologists

Skill Level (n)	Average Sales Revenue (1987)	Ratio between Levels	Average Age	Average Years in Practice
AAA (0)	n/a	n/a	n/a	n/a
AA (3)	$4,200,000	3.23	n/a	13
A (5)	$1,300,000	3.9	43	9
Rookie (5)	$330,000	1	40	14

Note: n/a expresses the fact that there were no Triple A clients in this system at the time. Adapted from William R. Torbert, *The Balance of Power, Transforming Self, Society, and Scientific Inquiry* (Newbury Park, CA: Sage Publications, 1991), 55.

staffs, with oversight—can see essentially three patients at a time." Double As, "able to see critical gaps in services, move into unoccupied niches, and create contracts that motivate partner physicians—are able to create multi-site practices and see three times again as many patients."[20]

Our last example is drawn from entrepreneurs operating in a different industry. As Peter Corning explains in his book, *Holistic Darwinism*, the methods of mining changed significantly over the five-year period from 1848 to 1853 that marked the California gold rush.[21] The four major shifts he describes reflect various levels of innovation and the large differences in productivity that result. In the first year,

> the classic model of individual prospectors wading in mountain streams with tin pans was largely supplanted by three-man teams using shovels and "rocker boxes," an innovation that also increased the quantity of material that could be processed in a day from ten or fifteen buckets to more than one hundred buckets, or at least twice as much per man. Shortly thereafter, the wooden sluice made its appearance. Though it required six- to eight-man teams (with an associated ownership and management structure), a sluice could handle 400 to 500 buckets of material per day, or about twice as much per man as a rocker box.
>
> When hydraulic mining was introduced in 1853, teams of 25 or more men were required to process and haul the materials and manage the water pumps, hoses, etc., that were used to blast away the faces of entire hillsides. A relatively large amount of capital was also needed and an organization was required to manage the technology and the large workforce. However, the amount of material processed daily also jumped to one hundred tons or more.[22]

The application of our framework to this example suggests that the individual prospectors were Rookie entrepreneurs; the three-man teams using rocker-boxes were Single As; the six-to-eight man teams using wood sluices were Double As; and, the hydraulic mining companies were started by Triple As. The skills necessary to develop and commercialize each subsequent technology represented the next level in the skill ladder. And each higher innovation was associated with at least a doubling in productivity per person (see Table 3.6).

The financial, market and competitive implications of these productivity improvements on the value of the firms operating at the higher skill levels were significant.

TABLE 3.6.
Gold Mining Productivity by Innovation and Skill Level

Skill Level	Approach and Technology	Output	Productivity per Man
AAA	Hydraulic technology utilizing teams of 25	100 tons or more a day	Doubled
AA	Six- to eight-man teams using wood sluices	400–500 buckets a day	Doubled
A	Three-man teams using rocker boxes	100 buckets a day	Doubled
Rookie	Individual prospectors using shovels	10–15 buckets a day	

Adapted from Peter A. Corning, *Holistic Darwinism* (Chicago: University of Chicago Press, 2005), 119.

Without reference to the ladder of skill, the dramatic differences in results offered in these four examples would be inexplicable and astounding. Instead, they reveal a pattern of changes in outcomes that suggest that the returns to higher skill levels are not incremental, but rather, real, substantial, nonlinear, and transformational.

WHAT DO ENTREPRENEURS SAY ABOUT SKILL LEVELS?

Finally, we would like to report on what the entrepreneurs, the subjects of these stories, have to say about skill levels. The first time we ever applied these skill levels was with a minority business incubation program in West Philadelphia that we were responsible for designing. At that time, back in 1996, we had not yet developed the assessment tools that we now utilize, and a group of us who knew the entrepreneurs made a judgment on the basis of our experience and impressions. Prior to meeting with each client to discuss our assessment, some of us were quite nervous about the possibility of conflicting perceptions, particularly if the client felt they were more skillful than we did.

Much to our surprise, 29 out of the 30 entrepreneurs agreed completely with our assessments, and the disagreement with the 30th entrepreneur was slight and a matter of judgment; either of us could have been right (we thought he was a high-level Rookie and he thought he was a low-level Single A). But what came as a shock to us was the emotional reaction of the entrepreneurs: every single one of them expressed to us that they were *relieved* to find out their skill level. After asking for clarification, one entrepreneur, Andrea (not her real name), summed it up best with this story of her experience:

> I've been participating in this incubation program for two years now. Every day, I've been coming in, working diligently on my business, and making what I thought was slow, but steady progress. Then, about six months ago, Leslie (not her real name) entered the program. In about six months, she went from 0 to 7 employees and from no sales to more than $750,000 in revenue. Her business was busting at the seams; she is ready to graduate and move out of here to a larger space of her own. All of the while, I've been asking myself—so what's the matter with me? Why is that not happening to me?

This entrepreneur's experience of watching another go through the process in what seemed to be record time was unnerving and shook her self-confidence. What Andrea learned from the assessment process was that she was a Rookie and that Leslie was a Double A (who had started several other businesses before)—a difference of two skill levels. One would naturally expect a more skillful and experienced entrepreneur to be able to go through the startup phases of a business more quickly than a novice. Once Andrea understood the reason for that difference (a difference she had observed but didn't know how to make sense of), she was relieved. She now had an explanation that didn't mean there was something wrong with her. Instead there was an objective difference, about which she had the power to do something.

Andrea now watched everything Leslie did with new eyes, as an example of what she could become, if and when she developed the necessary skills. As the other entrepreneurs in the program also reported, their thinking changed during this assessment process. Now they asked themselves: "if that person can do it, why can't I? What I need to do is watch, listen and learn." With the introduction of these explicit reference points—where one stands relative to different levels of performance—a dynamic force for positive change was unleashed in the incubator.

When we have introduced the Skill Ladder and the Pipeline to hundreds of entrepreneurs of various types and in different parts of the world over the past 15 years, the response has always been the same: entrepreneurs find the Skill Ladder to be an intellectually and emotionally satisfying framework, because it helps make sense of their experiences

TABLE 3.7.
Composite Table Describing Performance Ratios among Skill Levels across Four Analyses

Analyses: Skill Level	Advantage Valley ELS® (N = 73)	ELS® of Central Louisiana (N = 109)	Entrepreneurial Ophthalmologists (N = 13)	Gold-Mining Entrepreneurs* (N = n/a)
AAA	n/a	n/a	n/a	Doubled
AA	1.6	4.9	3.23	Doubled
A	6.0	2.3	3.9	Doubled
Rookie	1.0	1.0	1.0	1.0

*The gold-mining example represents per-man productivity increase, not the increase in company sales revenue, as in the case of the other three columns. *Note*: n/a expresses the fact that there were no Triple A clients in this system at the time.

in a positive and empowering way. It also helps them situate themselves with respect to others (e.g., through points of comparison or reference) and gives them a greater understanding of the challenges they are facing; challenges that they learn are not just unique to them, but are a natural part of the process of developing skills. The responses of entrepreneurs lead us to believe that the Skill Ladder is capturing differences that are real.[23] Entrepreneurs are able to see themselves and their history reflected in the Skill Ladder.

Is there a relationship between skill and performance? The data clearly suggests that the answer is yes (see Table 3.7).

From this analysis, we conclude that the higher the level of entrepreneurial skill, the greater the business assets and wealth that will be created. This is an important determination, because in our globally competitive economy, as Geoff Colvin, a former Fortune magazine editor argues, "the costs of being less than truly world class are growing, as are the rewards of being genuinely great."[24]

HOW ARE SKILLS DEVELOPED?

The Most Important Insight

The most powerful and important insight of this work is that *developing new skills or moving from one skill level to another requires a transformation in the abilities of the entrepreneur.* In other words, moving from one level to another isn't an incremental change—it is a major shift, one that involves a fundamental reorganization of an individual's previous knowledge, as well as of the structure of his thinking and behavior. It is a qualitative, not a quantitative, change, and that is what accounts for the large, often nonlinear differences in performance.

How does this kind of a change occur? An entrepreneur, whose skills we had assessed at the Single A level more than two years earlier, finally decided to participate in the coaching program we offer. We insisted that she be reassessed, but she objected, saying: "It's been two years since the first assessment; I must be at least a Double A by now." The new assessment, to which she reluctantly consented, indicated that she was still a Single A, and we placed her on a team consisting of other Single As. When she continued to protest, we made a deal with her: "if after participating in the first meeting with the 11 other entrepreneurs on this team, you feel that you are not in their league, that you do not belong and don't feel comfortable, we will gladly place you on a team of Double A entrepreneurs." After that meeting, she reported to us that this team was where she belonged. Some were slightly above her in their skills and some slightly below, but overall they were all at the same level of development.

This thinking, which is all too common, reflects the belief that developing skills, like the growth rings of a tree, occurs inevitably with the passage of time as in the process of maturation. It is not like that. There is nothing inevitable or automatic about the development of higher-level skills. The shifts required to move up a skill level are "discontinuous," meaning not more of the same (which represents a continuous change, a change that takes place within an existing structure), but something fundamentally different, representing a change in structure. Let's illustrate with an example.

Nowhere are the differences in skill levels among entrepreneurs as clear as in the case of how they understand their markets. When you get to the bottom of the thinking that actually drives a Rookie's behavior, a good customer is a warm body—simply a living, breathing person. Unfortunately, it takes a Single A to realize that a warm body is no good unless they have money in their pockets that they are willing to spend on what you have to offer.

Rookies tend to lead with the features of their product or service. They approach their customers from the inside out. Whether consciously or not (and few are conscious of their internal thought processes), they say to themselves *"I think this is the greatest product, and so should you."* A Rookie's selection of offerings is often based on whether or not they themselves would be willing to buy it; they never consider whether or not they are representative of other customers out there. They have a "build it and they will come" mentality.

By the time one gets to the Double A level (and note that there is a transitional level in between that we are skipping over for the moment), the priority in thinking has shifted from the features of the product to the value of this offering to the customer. In other words, Double As (and the skill levels above them) approach their customers from the outside in. They say to themselves, "given what you, the customer, need or want, my offering should be of unique value to you."

This fundamental shift in thinking—from the inside-out of the Rookie to the outside-in of the Double A and higher, is not achieved by increasing the amount of marketing information that the entrepreneur is given or which he absorbs. It is not achieved by having them do a marketing plan. As we like to say, no matter how much more information you shove into their head, it will not change what goes on between their ears!

This kind of shift can only be achieved by fundamentally changing one's way of thinking, in this case, from the inside-out to the outside-in. As one of our coaches is fond of saying, "Rookies need, but rarely have, out-of-body experiences." But when they do, it marks their shift to the Single A level, because it makes it possible for them to truly restructure their thinking.

Similar discontinuous changes can be seen in sports as well. Twice in his life, Tiger Woods, one of the world's top golfers, significantly changed his swing in order to take his play to a higher level. Each change was a transformation, because it required him to reorganize and restructure everything about his game. For a period of time, before he mastered his new swing, his new performance was worse than his previous level of achievement. Yet by persisting with his practice, he was able to move to the next level of skill and significantly change his competitive position.

Transformational or discontinuous changes involve substantial challenges and risks. "Suppose you want to lower your average golf score from 95 to 90. This can probably be accomplished by practicing more often. But, lowering your score to the 80s is an entirely different story, because to do so will involve unlearning many procedures that inhibit your progress. Unfortunately, while being involved in this 'relearning' process, you will be risking that your score might rise to 125!"[25]

Having to unlearn what you previously had to learn in order to get where you are is a challenge in and of itself. The risk is that the decline in performance an entrepreneur experiences as he absorbs new knowledge and skills will not be short-term. That is why, to reduce that risk, almost all high-level performers seek and receive help.

IMPLICATIONS FOR DEVELOPING SKILLS

Skill mastery has many levels to it. You don't become a master from a novice in one jump, nor can you skip individual levels. There are significant steps in between that must be negotiated. Each level, like belts in the martial arts, is built upon another and proceeds in a discrete and conceptually manageable way.

This means that the material in any "curriculum" for mastering entrepreneurial skills must be organized by levels. Otherwise the development process will be both inefficient and ineffective, with material being presented in the wrong order and at the wrong time. We have witnessed numerous training programs that violate this design principle, largely because they assume that every individual has the same capability, and the only thing they lack is information.

One of us once attended an entrepreneurship conference and watched in amazement as the Rookies in the room tried to absorb the speaker's lessons on branding, a subject that is only appropriate to entrepreneurs at the Double A level and above. You could literally see their eyes glaze over as they struggled unsuccessfully to understand how to relate this information to their business. (Using that physiological response alone as a rough indicator, we estimated that more than 50 percent of the participants were Rookies.) As we pointed out in the story that began this chapter, the lack of understanding about the audience's skill level results in an extremely inefficient use of scarce resources, including, and most important from the clients' point of view, their time. The implication is that many of our programs for educating entrepreneurs need to be redesigned to help them with the right knowledge at the right time.

One of the observations we made earlier in this chapter is that variations in skill level require us to work with entrepreneurs at each level quite differently. To take a very simple contrast, working with Rookies is very hands-on; in some cases, it requires supervised, "on-the-job" training for certain tasks to be effective. On the other hand, one can merely describe the idea or process to a Double A and they will be able to figure out how to apply it to their situation. However, most entrepreneurship training programs are designed as classroom sessions, are oriented to abstract principles, and leave participants on their own to figure out how to apply the material. There is nothing wrong with that approach if the participants are Double As; for Rookies, the material might be great, but the approach will certainly lose them. Again, it is not a question of the content, but of the way in which it is delivered, and its appropriateness to that particular skill level.

IT'S NOT ABOUT TALENT

Researchers who have spent the last 20 years studying expertise in a wide variety of fields—from sports, to music, to science and commerce—have come to a myth-busting conclusion: talent is clearly over-rated as an explanation of world-class performance. Two recent books, *Talent Is Overrated* and *The Talent Code,* describe their findings.[26] What distinguishes the world-class performers from the average person is how much and how *well* they practice. Researchers have even determined the average number of hours of practice that leads to mastery in any field: 10,000 hours. Given that we have other things to do in our lives, this usually takes even the most dedicated individuals at least 10 years of intensive study to achieve. One author summed up what he calls the universal theory of skills in one brief equation: "Deep practice x 10,000 hours = world-class skill."[27]

What do these researchers mean by deep or "deliberate" practice? Deliberate practice is an activity specifically designed to continuously improve performance. It involves:

- A strategic choice of what to practice—well-defined elements that need to be improved. Focusing on correcting mistakes and errors; insistently seeking out what one is not good at.
- Stretching beyond one's current abilities; operating at the edge, outside of one's comfort zone.
- Intense attention. The mentally demanding effort involved in focusing and concentrating is what makes this kind of practice "deliberate" as opposed to mindless activity.
- A mind-boggling amount of repetition, until the behavior becomes fluid, can be performed with a high degree of accuracy as well as consistency, and can be done without conscious effort. At this

point, one can stop attending to the mechanics and start thinking about the application or strategy.

- Continuous feedback on results, which usually requires a teacher, mentor or coach: someone who can provide a clear and unbiased view of the subject's performance and can see them in ways they cannot see themselves.

In short, there are requirements to get to a level of mastery.

WHAT ABOUT MOZART AND STEVE JOBS?

You might ask how these discoveries account for people like Mozart, Bill Gates, and Steve Jobs? Mozart was certainly a child prodigy, wasn't he? Interestingly enough, the life stories of these individuals in no way violate these rules of skill development. In fact, they conform very nicely to them.

While Mozart did compose and perform at an early age, he did not become world famous until after he reached the age of 21, when he had put in more than 10,000 hours of practice. More importantly, by the standards of most music critics, the compositions he wrote when he was young were not exceptional; none of those pieces are being listened to today. It is only the music he composed after the age of 21 that is considered to be exceptional in its quality.[28]

Similarly, by the time Bill Gates was 21, he had over 10,000 hours of computer programming experience. This was unusual for his age, but it fits the pattern of what occurs in other fields.[29]

As for Steve Jobs, we would like to offer an alternative interpretation of what has become the myth about a truly exceptional and successful Major League entrepreneur. It is this: Steve Jobs (and, we can't forget, Steve Wozniak) started Apple Computing and took it to a certain level of success, but the company stalled out, we would argue, because of his skill limitations as an entrepreneur. While we are speculating here, let us say that he was overall a Double A entrepreneur (perhaps a Triple A or higher in terms of his entrepreneurial skills, with probably a much lower level of management skills, which resulted in an average score across all dimensions at the Double A level). He was kicked out by his board. Why? We think it was because he lacked those higher-level management skills. In our judgment, he was a person with brilliant product ideas, but with significant deficiencies in his ability to build Apple into a consistently profitable business asset.

Jobs left and started Next Computing as well as Pixar, both significant efforts. During this time, he developed his managerial "chops," those deficient skills, and he was asked to return to the helm of Apple in 1996 as a Major League entrepreneur. Steve Jobs was clearly not born a Major League entrepreneur. He started out, like everyone else, as a Rookie entrepreneur, a member of a computer club. He developed enormously as an entrepreneur during his first tenure at Apple. But he had to leave the company in order to develop his skills further and demonstrate, as a result of his experience with his other ventures, that he had developed sufficiently to lead Apple to the next level in terms of its growth as a business.

What is most interesting to us, and what we think tends to support this interpretation of his story, is what Jobs did first when he returned to Apple. As McGrath and MacMillan, two entrepreneurship scholars and educators, explain, "Although Apple has always been known for highly innovative and stylish products, a key underpinning for its turnaround after founder Steve Jobs returned to the company in 1996 was a renewed focus on efficiency and operations."[30] They go on to quote a 2000 *Business Week* cover story:

> Get a load of this: The company known for its incorrigible, free-spirited, free-spending ways has become a master of operating efficiencies. Jobs has slashed expenses from $8.1 billion in 1997 to $5.7 billion in 1999 by outsourcing manufacturing, trimming inventories, shifting 25% of sales to an online store, and slicing the number of distributors from the double digits to two. That, combined with the new products, has won back allies.[31]

The successful management of the business as a system of asset portfolios required that he do this. We believe the process of developing these skills took at least 10 years and more than 10,000 hours.

THE BIOLOGICAL BASIS OF SKILLS

Researchers have also found a biological basis for the development of skills: myelin. The physiological foundation of skills is "built on three simple facts.

1. Every human movement, thought, or feeling is a precisely timed electric signal traveling through a chain of neurons—a circuit of nerve fibers.
2. Myelin is the insulation that wraps these nerve fibers and increases signal strength, speed, and accuracy.
3. The more we fire a particular circuit, the more myelin optimizes that circuit, and the stronger, faster, and more fluent our movements and thoughts become."[32]

The process by which we develop skills is grounded in our physiology. "The 10 year, 10,000 hour rule has more universal implications. It implies that all skills are built using the same fundamental mechanism and further that the mechanism involves physiological limits from which no one is exempt."[33]

SUPPORTING SKILL DEVELOPMENT

Skill development doesn't just happen in isolation. Negotiating these challenges is extremely difficult and requires help. For example, even pro golfers still go to teachers, as do athletes in every sport. The question is, what kind of help do they need?

The monumental nature of the tasks confronting the entrepreneur requires the abilities of a coach or mentor, as distinct from a consultant. In our experience, there is an important difference between coaching and consulting. Consultants provide expertise in solving problems on a discrete basis, within the scope of an engagement or transaction. Coaches, over the course of a long-term relationship, help entrepreneurs see their need for expert assistance and help prepare them to use a consultant's expertise. That is not the role of a consultant. There are rare individuals that can do both; but it is important to understand that they are performing two different functions, both of which are important.[34]

We are not saying that absolutely anyone can be an entrepreneur, just as not everyone is equally capable of performing every job, like a salesperson, computer programmer, or graphic designer. But the myth about the importance of talent to success is dangerous. Why? Because it gives us an excuse; it allows us to say, "I can never make it because I don't have the talent." Such excuses block us from the truth: that by deliberately developing our skills, we can achieve great things.

CONCLUSION

The first key variable in the Pipeline of Entrepreneurs and Enterprises is entrepreneurship skills. A skill can be defined as the ability to perform a particular action or task on a consistent basis, at a high level of performance, without a great deal of conscious thinking or attention, to achieve a desired outcome. We maintain that success in entrepreneurship requires the mastery of a skill set, that entrepreneurs come to entrepreneurship at different levels of skill, and that these skills can be developed.

The skill set that all entrepreneurs must master can be described as including four chief dimensions: technical, managerial, entrepreneurial, and personal maturity skills. Entrepreneurs can be classified according to their level of skill across these dimensions. We use the American baseball farm system as our metaphor for classifying entrepreneurs on the rungs of a Ladder of Skills.

Our field research has permitted us to verify the existence of these distinct levels of entrepreneurship skill, to demonstrate that movement from one skill level to the next-highest level requires a transformation in thought and understanding, and to document that advances in skill level correlate with substantial increases in business revenue generated. The research of others shows that the ability to develop one's skills is rooted in both physiology and long-term practice. We believe that the best way to facilitate skill building in entrepreneurs is through coaching, which prepares the entrepreneur to make better use of consulting and other more traditional forms of entrepreneurship assistance.

In the next chapter, we will discuss the other key variable in the Pipeline—the stage in a business's life cycle.

Categorizing Entrepreneurs According to Their Goals

Many policymakers tend to classify entrepreneurs into types according to their goals. After reviewing a range of existing classifications, we have identified four distinct types of business goals:

1. *Survival* (more commonly called Necessity): for example, traditional small business—constrained view of the possibilities. Often focused on income or job substitution.

2. *Lifestyle:* hobby, control over time (leisure), passive investment—similarly constrained view of business possibilities but for different reasons.

3. *Growth* or asset creation: classic entrepreneurship (referred to by the Global Entrepreneurship Monitor [GEM] as Opportunity entrepreneurship).[35]

   • Competitive: pursuing a gap in the marketplace
   • Productive: pursuing an opportunity for innovation

4. *Missionary:* could be social, public or private objectives—for example, to put a computer in every home (Jobs and Wozniak), or a car in every garage (Henry Ford).

While goals are an important factor in entrepreneurship, we do not believe that it is a relevant method for sorting entrepreneurs. As a filter for decision making, it can lead to seriously distorted conclusions. For example, everyone wants more "growth" firms in their communities. Therefore, the thinking goes, we need to find more "growth" entrepreneurs. No one is very clear about how to do this, but people seem to be very quick to make judgments about who is or isn't a growth entrepreneur and confident about their decisions to give or withhold available resources on the basis of their judgments. We however, are not so confident in their judgments or in our ability to make such judgments. Because we are not, we suggest an alternative.

Our focus as economic developers should not be to find more growth entrepreneurs, but instead to help influence "survival" entrepreneurs to shift their goals from merely surviving to truly growing. We have managed to do this frequently in our coaching practice. In our experience, those entrepreneurs who are focused on survival are doing so because they don't know how to do anything else, nor do they have any idea that they can grow something bigger. They take their cues from their environment, and few of them have seen someone make a different choice (except perhaps in the media).

Entrepreneurs begin to change their goals after long-term exposure to other entrepreneurs, usually at the same skill level (and often from similar circumstances), who have made different choices and are experiencing success. When they see what another entrepreneur has accomplished, an entrepreneur who perhaps also did not finish college, or who came from the wrong side of the tracks, or who like themselves doesn't like public speaking, they usually respond by saying, "I never thought I could do that, but if he or she can, why can't I?"

In other words, entrepreneurs will make different choices when directly exposed to other reference points and possibilities (media images are not sufficient). If you've never actually seen someone do something, then it's hard to imagine that you can do it yourself. No one believed that the mile could be run in less than four minutes, until Roger Bannister, who wasn't considered among the world's top talents, became the first person in history to do it in 1954. Then within three years, 17 other people had accomplished the task also. After Bannister's success, the goal changed from being "impossible" to being possible.[36]

With respect to business, a European researcher has actually discovered a similar result: "if a new firm is exposed to growth oriented mental models early in its life [this should read "entrepreneur"], this is likely to install a growth-oriented ethos in the firm and lead to faster growth later in its life."[37]

The potentially faulty judgments from the use of goals as a classification method are not exclusive to the category of survival entrepreneurs. So called lifestyle entrepreneurs are referred to rather negatively by the economic development community, believing that their choice of business goal is a reflection of their limited ability as an entrepreneur or business person. Such a conclusion cannot possibly be justified on the basis of their choice of goals alone. At an age when most people retire, serial entrepreneurs are still starting businesses. Many of them choose to indulge in their hobbies and interests, business choices that will not necessarily lead to making much money (which they don't need) or result in the creation of many jobs. Does this mean that they are not serious, skilled entrepreneurs and as such don't represent a potential asset to the community?

There is no such thing as survival entrepreneurs or growth entrepreneurs, only entrepreneurs who have chosen survival or growth as a goal. We believe that people are using goals as a surrogate, lacking any better way to differentiate among entrepreneurs. But as these examples suggest, we must be cautious about making judgments on this basis. The labeling this classification method uses serves to diminish people, not to enable them. It assumes something that is inherently not true: that goals are fixed.

Goals are a matter of choice and are independent of the "type" of entrepreneur, who we believe is more effectively classified by skill level. Being a matter of choice, goals are also subject to change. Differentiating goals from, rather than conflating them with, other variables, such as the type of entrepreneur, gives us more options for building a better economy.

4

Stages in the Life Cycle of a Business

It is not the strongest of the species that survive, nor the most intelligent, but the ones most responsive to change.

—Charles Darwin

In this chapter, we examine the second key variable in the Pipeline of Entrepreneurs and Enterprises: the stages in the life cycle of the business (see Figure 4.1). We distinguish between the entrepreneur and the business; they are not one and the same. The business is a creation of the entrepreneur, a manifestation of the entrepreneur's goals and efforts. An entrepreneur can, and in many cases will, create many different businesses over the course of her lifetime. Often referred to as serial entrepreneurship, this pursuit of multiple business opportunities over time is a key to successfully building wealth.

It is equally possible for the business to exist independently of the entrepreneur who founded it, meaning that a single business can be run by different entrepreneurs over time. For our purposes, it is critical to separate the business from the entrepreneur, because the dynamics of the business are different from those of the entrepreneur. The business life cycle represents the horizontal dimension in our framework.

DEVELOPING AN ACTIONABLE MODEL OF THE BUSINESS LIFE CYCLE

Before developing our framework, we reviewed more than 26 different life cycle models.[1] In contrast to other model builders, our goal is

FIGURE 4.1.

Life Cycle Stages of the Business

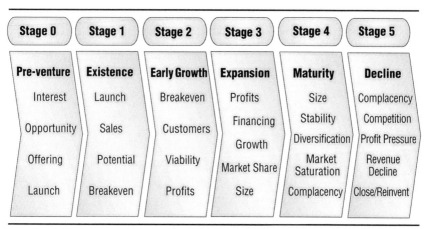

© Collaborative Strategies, LLC.

to learn how life cycle stages influence what entrepreneurs and their firms need, and specifically, not generically, what kind of help coaches, consultants, and advisers should be offering.

The existing models of the business life cycle we encountered were of limited value to us for a number of important reasons:

1. None of the models provided any operational definitions or determinants of stages. The boundaries between their stages are fuzzy. It is not made clear, in a precise way, when one stage ends and another begins. There is no way to determine what life cycle stage a particular business is actually in (a key requirement for our purposes). Instead, it is assumed that major differences in organizational structure, management challenges, or market position will make this obvious to actors and observers alike. Yet considerations of inter-rater reliability (i.e., whether anyone else would be able to rate that business similarly, using these definitions) have never appeared in any of the discussion of business life cycles, and this is a significant concern.

2. Most of the life cycle models are incomplete and inconsistent with respect to the level of detail across stages. For example, while half (13 of the 26 models examined) have a pre-venture stage(s), the others do not. A handful of these models have a decline or death

stage, but the majority do not. The high-technology-focused models place significant emphasis on the pre-venture stage, in some cases breaking it down into multiple substages, while paying little attention to the maturity or decline stages. These latter models appear to assume unending growth. Some models represent growth as being a staged process, but others jump immediately from startup into rapid growth.

3. Most models are specific to certain types of business and are not universal enough to be useful across various types of firms. While some may argue that this is justified by differences among types of ventures, we find that these differences are minor and largely artificial. If exceptions to the rules exist, then they need to be proven definitively. It is not sufficient to make unsubstantiated claims without providing evidence and argument/analysis to support them. In our experience, such supposed exceptions (e.g., technology firms that continue to exist ad infinitum in a stable state, or startups without the pre-venture stage) do not exist.

   However, having said that, we do believe that there must be issues that are unique to particular types of firms. It is just that what these are must be based on research or experience, as opposed to subjective speculation. A standard set of definitions would allow us to begin answering questions about which life cycle issues are indeed generic and which, if any, are specific to certain types of firms or businesses, or particular business designs, and so on.

4. All of the models are biased toward particular dimensions—the marketing dimension or the management dimension—and ignore all others. None are multidimensional across stages. These models are incapable of dealing with the possibility that a firm might be at one stage on one dimension, for example marketing, but at another stage in another dimension, such as human resources.

5. Many of these models confuse stages in the business life cycle with strategies. For example, diversification, harvest, and stability are not themselves stages (and yet were so identified in a number of cases), but strategies that may be pursued at various stages in the life cycle.

6. Most of these models are depictions of business *growth* patterns, not necessarily *development* patterns.

7. They blur the distinction between the entrepreneur and the business in ways that are not useful. The business is often described as if it is doing the acting. But a company cannot decide whether to grow or not; only the entrepreneur can make those decisions. The

entrepreneur's ability to do so is a critical determinant of the business's success.

For a model of the life cycle stages of a business to be useful for our purposes, not only does it need to address these limitations, it must also help us to:

- Accurately and consistently assess a business's stage in the life cycle[2]
- Diagnose the needs and issues businesses experience within particular stages, as well as across stages
- Articulate the change strategies entrepreneurs can and have used to successfully move their business from one stage to another
- Effectively match existing interventions with a firm's needs at a particular stage in its life cycle or design new interventions

STAGES IN THE LIFE CYCLE OF THE BUSINESS

With the goal of addressing these limitations, we have developed and implemented an actionable model of the six stages in the life cycle of a business. The following description summarizes our definition of the life cycle stages. Much of the material in the following subsections is quoted from the authors' 2006 article.[3]

Stage 0: Pre-Venture

"This phase begins with either an interest or desire on the part of an entrepreneur to start a business or an idea for a business, and it ends with the emergence/birth of an organization with an economic offering (i.e., a product or a service) ready to be sold to a potential client and generate revenue. During this founding or embryonic period, the groundwork necessary for a successful launch is laid."

The crucial activities or substages that are typically performed during this period include:

1. Contemplating the possibility of starting and/or owning a business
2. Searching for an idea and exploring various business possibilities

3. Selecting a particular opportunity and assessing its feasibility
4. Committing to a business by assuming risk and making investments of time, resources, and money
5. Developing an economic offering and a strategy
6. Launching the organization—including assembling the initial team

Stage 1: Existence or Infancy

"This phase begins when the business is launched (with a product or service ready for sale) and ends when the business has reached breakeven from sales (i.e., revenues minus expenses equal zero). The business has passed the first test of survival—its offering has demonstrated some interest by a small set of customers, although acceptance by the 'market' has not yet been demonstrated. Profitability has not yet been achieved and the venture's continued viability (i.e., its ability to maintain a separate existence) is not assured. However, the business exhibits potential."

Stage 2: Early Growth

"This phase begins with breakeven from sales and, if successful, ends with the establishment of a sustainable business—with either healthy or marginal profits. The latter pays a living wage (i.e., a mom and pop operation), while the former would be positioned to grow further." In part, which of these two options occurs is a function of the entrepreneur's skill level and goals, as described in the sidebar in chapter 3. "This level of economic viability or measure of stability has been achieved by securing and satisfying a critical mass of customers and producing sufficient cash flow to at least repair and replace the capital assets necessary to continue the business as they wear out. This assures the survival of the business, as long as market conditions remain the same."

Stage 3: Expansion or Sustained Growth

"This stage begins when a business, with healthy profits and a clear indication of growth potential, marshals its resources for growth by risking the established borrowing or equity power of the business to finance growth (even if profitable, cash flow is typically insufficient to supply the needed growth capital for the next phase). This stage ends when the company has emerged as a growth business, has demonstrated the capability to serve many customers, has delivered a variety of products and services, has grown quickly, has operated profitably, has captured market share, has successfully defended against competitors, and has expanded operations and sustained increases in growth and profitability over time. If successful, the business will reach a size that is sufficiently large, given its industry and market niche, to earn a significant economic return on its assets and labor."

Stage 4: Maturity

"This phase begins when the company has 'arrived'—it has successfully achieved the advantages of size and stability, a strong market position (e.g., share of the market), a strong level of profitability, positive cash flow and a strong management team with an effective system of controls in place. Growth (including the growth 'rate'), however, has slowed and market saturation as well as competitive pressures are on the horizon. The challenge of this phase is to avoid ossification and decline by resisting complacency and preserving or re-establishing the firm's entrepreneurial spirit. If it has not already done so, it is important that the company make the transition from a single product line company to a multi-product company as well as from a single business to a more diversified but complementary multi-business unit operation. To continue to thrive, the company must maintain a dynamic balance between conserving existing assets and pursuing new market opportunities. This phase begins to end (not all at once) when the balance favors the status quo, even in the face of an increasingly competitive environment."

Stage 5: Decline

"This phase begins when, due to complacency and a desire to avoid risk, market share begins to decline, cash flow and profitability, while still adequate, begin to deteriorate from competitive pressures and the company begins to feed off of its accumulated assets. This phase ends when the company is either sold, closed or manages to reinvent itself—usually through the replacement of the management team."

CRITICAL OBSERVATIONS ABOUT LIFE CYCLE STAGES

The following observations are crucial to understanding the life cycle itself, and its relevance to business development.

The development of the business is a process that takes place over time and through distinct stages. Each stage in the life cycle makes certain demands on a business—demands which, if ignored or violated, contribute to a firm's failure. For example, each stage in the life cycle of a business has very different operating requirements. These systems must change as the business goes through its life cycle. An accounting system provides a simple illustration. Pre-venture companies can, in many cases, survive with an accounting system that operates out of a shoebox. Such a process would be unthinkable for a company in the Early Growth or Expansion stages. Similarly, the selection of an accounting package with high administrative demands, suitable for a business in the Maturity stage, could cause an Existence or Early Growth stage company to go bankrupt due to the exorbitant overhead requirements.

Movement from one stage to the next stage in the life cycle requires a transformation in the operations. It is a whole new ball game at each stage in the life cycle, as many entrepreneurs are quite surprised to discover—because they are not familiar with the different phases of the journey and how the terrain changes. The behavior that successfully got an entrepreneur to one stage, may, if he continues doing what he did before, be the cause of his failure at another. For example, when the firm is small, the entrepreneur can personally touch all of the customers and all of the transactions. As it grows too large for one person to perform the work, he has to find other ways to know and control what is going on. One entrepreneur, with whom we have worked, successfully grew his business from $75,000 to $425,000 in revenue and moved from the Existence stage to the Early Growth stage. Now he is essentially operating an entirely new business. The behavior that brought him to his current stage (taking charge, doing things himself, making decisions on gut instinct, etc.) will not only *not* be successful as he tries to move to the Expansion stage, it will destroy his business. The changes that must be negotiated from stage to stage are not smooth and linear; they are in fact qualitatively different as well as discontinuous, and this is one of the most important lessons entrepreneurs must learn.

A transformation is not the same as growth, which is an increase in scale without a change in structure. A business that attempts to grow without changing its structure in accordance with the demands of that stage in the life cycle will simply die. "Another example in which physical limits are set by the laws of nature is found in scaling. Though a few economists believe that a machine can be built twice as big without changing production functions, according to the laws of nature you can neither scale up nor down at will. To build a bigger machine than has been built to date you know beforehand that limits will have to be overcome by the discovery of stronger materials. This discovery was made by Galileo, who, in his *Two Sciences,* showed why it was impossible to imagine one dog exactly twice as large as another without it having strong bones."[4] Such changes are not necessarily smooth.

Stages cannot be skipped, although a firm can move into decline from any stage. Some people believe that certain rules of growth or development do not apply to "special" categories such as technology companies; that they are somehow exceptions to the life cycle process. However, this thinking is finally changing, as Geoffrey Moore, a leading technology consultant, observes, "because the technology sector is becoming more like the rest of the economy. No longer does anyone think technology companies are exempt from the laws of gravity. No longer are words like consolidation, commoditization, legacy, and inertia inapplicable to the sector. The sector is coming of age."[5]

Successful movement through these stages is not inevitable. Death can occur at any stage, or a firm's progression can become arrested at a particular stage. Many life cycle models seem to give the illusion that the business has a life or reality of its own and that it will proceed inexorably and inevitably at its own pace through the stages, independent of the entrepreneur. Furthermore, these models imply that it is up to the entrepreneur to adjust his or her management style or marketing strategy accordingly. This could not be further from the truth. As we will explain more fully in Chapter 6, it is the entrepreneur's appropriate skill set and business goals that determine if, when, and how the enterprise will advance through its life cycle stages.

Growth within a particular life cycle stage can be accelerated up to a point, but it is difficult to do this effectively without damaging the firm's long-term probabilities for success. This is a motivation of certain stakeholders, like venture capitalists, who want to cash out on their investment as quickly as possible.

A business's life cycle stage is not identical with, nor can it be identified by, the age of the firm. Many companies are 30 years old and arrested in an early stage of development. Regarding the assumption that gazelles (high-growth companies that are the new target of all economic development organizations) are all young, David Birch (a business researcher) finds that they are generally somewhat older than most small companies. Although some businesses take off like rockets almost from birth, the more common pattern is a "gradual development phase followed by a robust (but not explosive) growth." Nearly one-fifth of gazelles have been in operation 30 years or more.[6]

It is at the stages of Expansion or Sustained Growth (3) and Maturity (4) that substantial, long-lasting assets and wealth get created, and a significant number of jobs are generated. It is also at this stage that owners can become philanthropists and begin to contribute to their community financially and as civic leaders. In the debate between the two positions of business attraction (which focuses economic development activities on large, existing companies) and growth from within, it is frequently forgotten that the large firms with which we are so enamored were once small, and all were founded or launched by entrepreneurs, as noted in Chapter 1. These large businesses are the result of a long period of gestation and multiple stages of development. Ignoring the time dimension leads us to expect unrealistic results, in shorter time periods and at earlier stages in the life cycle. Evaluating an early-stage firm on its rate of job creation or sales revenue is equivalent to judging a child on how fast he runs the 100-yard dash.

Entrepreneurship and innovation are important at every stage in the life cycle of a business, although the issues differ at each stage. For example, the need for line extensions or complementary products is an entrepreneurial issue that is unique to the expansion stage. Similarly, the issue of launching new ventures on entirely different business models within a parent company is exclusive to mature companies or those in need of reinventing themselves.[7]

Knowledge of the life cycle stages of a business is critical to understanding the development issues a firm is facing. The demands of each stage are quite different, as are the types of assistance firms needs. All of these issues are quite independent of the entrepreneur. In the next chapter, we will examine how these variables—entrepreneurial skills and life cycle stages—are put together to assemble a Pipeline of Entrepreneurs and Enterprises.

5

Moving from a Pool
to a Pipeline

In all affairs, it's a healthy thing now and then to hang a question mark on the things you have long taken for granted.

—Bertrand Russell

In this chapter, we examine how the variables we have discussed so far are put together to assemble a Pipeline of Entrepreneurs and Enterprises.

Before pioneers can settle a land, they must first map it. Without a map we are lost. Researchers at the Max Planck Institute for Biological Cybernetics in Germany found that when people get lost in the woods or in the desert and are without any reference points like the sun or a distant mountain, they walk in circles.[1] The Pipeline gives economic developers concrete reference points for managing the community's supply of entrepreneurs and enterprises, eliminating unproductive activity.

We chose a Pipeline as the most effective way to represent the territory we are exploring. It is also an extremely powerful visual metaphor. For us, the Pipeline brings to mind an image of a conduit, in the sense of "deal" flow in the venture capital or banking communities as well as one's "prospect list" in sales. While industrial or mechanical in nature, it captures the ideas of volume, or stocks, and flows as well as the processes of filtering or sorting, refining and purifying, as substances move through an extensive network or infrastructure of channels.

Most existing data on entrepreneurship are based on an analysis of a pool—an undifferentiated or homogeneous population of individuals.[2] Statistical analysis of this data can be used to describe an average population, but that tells us nothing about individuals, their needs, or how those needs can be met. The pool is a mass market. Efforts focused on a mass market may only reach some of that market or none at all.

Existing segmentations of population and economic data are limited in their usefulness for action, because they are not describing real entities. We may learn something about the profile of an average female-owned business, or the median profitability of a business in the computer sector located in an inner-city market, but these statistics give us no insight as to how to help those firms.

We seek to break free of the one-dimensional, flatland world[3] of the population pool, to a richer, multidimensional world. We want to go beyond correlating single variables with individual outcomes and instead explore how these independent variables are related to one another; to go from a statistical analysis to a structural representation. Most importantly, we want the knowledge we discover to be actionable, not merely descriptive. To achieve this, we needed a more highly differentiated lens or prism through which to examine this territory. We had to move from a pool to a Pipeline.

CONSTRUCTING A PIPELINE

Successfully navigating through physical space requires a map that represents all three dimensions—longitude, latitude, and altitude. Neither current nor desired position can be located with a single coordinate, nor can one dimension sufficiently represent the nature of the entrepreneurial assets in a community. Three dimensions or elements must be assembled together in a particular relationship to one another to give us a picture of the whole.

The Pipeline utilizes three dimensions to map the community's entrepreneurs and enterprises:

- The vertical dimension represents the five rungs in the skill ladder.
- The horizontal dimension represents the six life cycle stages of the business.
- The depth dimension represents the quantity of entrepreneurs and/or enterprises that occupy a particular segment of the Pipeline. This is symbolized by a number in the two-dimensional representation of the Pipeline or by the height of the bar in a three-dimensional representation.

Figure 5.1 illustrates how these three dimensions are assembled graphically into a template for the Pipeline, with the blanks repre-

FIGURE 5.1.
The Pipeline of Entrepreneurs and Enterprises

LIFE CYCLE STAGES
Stage 0
Pre-Venture
Stage 1
Existence
Stage 2
Early Growth
Stage 3
Expansion
Stage 4
Maturity
Stage 5
Decline
SKILL LEVELS
Major Leaguer
AAA
AA
A
Rookie

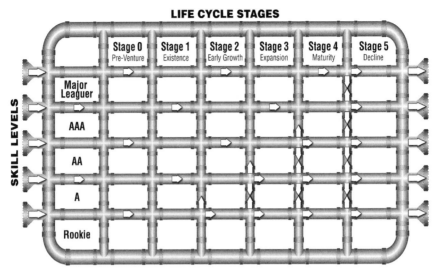

© Collaborative Strategies, LLC

FIGURE 5.2.
Two-Dimensional Representation of the Pipeline of Entrepreneurs and Enterprises

LIFE CYCLE STAGES
Stage 0
Pre-Venture
Stage 1
Existence
Stage 2
Early Growth
Stage 3
Expansion
Stage 4
Maturity
Stage 5
Decline
SKILL LEVELS
Major Leaguer
1
2
4
5
7
1
AAA
12
9
16
22
30
11
AA
30
69
24
96
35
12
A
45
53
150
6
0
3
Rookie
12
45
5
0
0
7

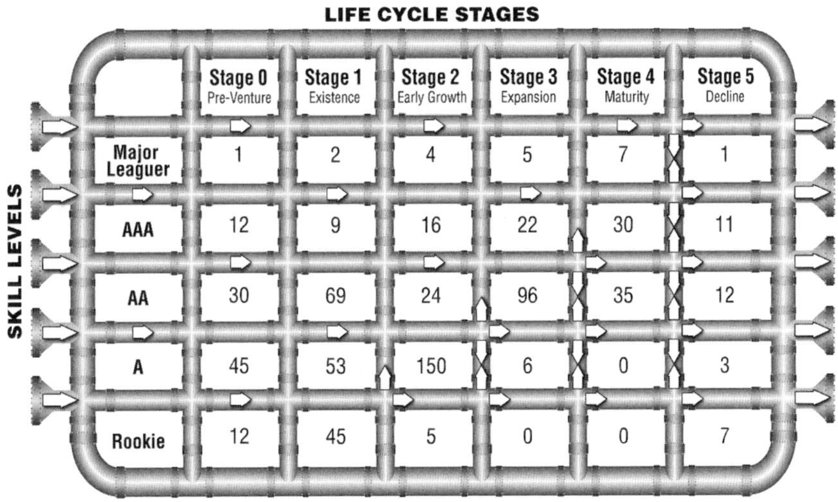

Note: The individual cells in this example represent the number of enterprises in the community in that segment of the Pipeline.
© Collaborative Strategies, LLC.

senting the spaces to indicate the quantity of entrepreneurs and/or enterprises in that particular segment. We now have a new lens through which we can see a Pipeline of variegated stocks and flows, instead of an undifferentiated pool. The following Pipeline, shown in Figure 5.2, is a two-dimensional representation of the volume and flow of entrepreneurial activity in a sample community. Figure 5.3 offers a three-dimensional presentation of that same information.

FIGURE 5.3.
Three-Dimensional Representation of the Pipeline of Entrepreneurs and Enterprises

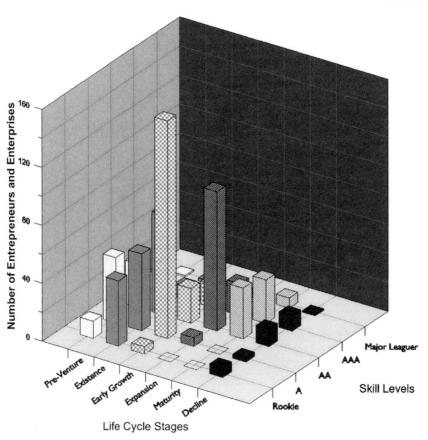

© Collaborative Strategies, LLC.

UNDERSTANDING PIPELINE ACTIVITY

These Pipeline diagrams enable us to answer the following questions about what is occurring in a community's economy:

- What is the volume—the number or quantity of stock—of entrepreneurs and enterprises in the Pipeline? In other words, how big is the pipe and what is its capacity? What percentage of the total population does this represent?
- What is the distribution of entrepreneurs and enterprises in the various segments of the Pipeline?
- What is the rate of flow of entrepreneurs and enterprises through the Pipeline as a whole on an annual basis? For example, what is the absolute number of new firms that are started, or that move to the area from elsewhere? How many business closures are there? What is the rate of business sales to existing entrepreneurs who want to start or buy a new business? What do these numbers represent as a percentage of the total Pipeline volume?
- What is the rate of movement between segments of the Pipeline? These figures represent the rate of transformation and indicate the change in the quality of the volume or stock. What is the rate of other outcomes—such as stagnation, exit, and death—by individual segment?
- What are the most common patterns of movement in the Pipeline in this community? Where are things stuck? Where are things flowing? Many Pipelines are poorly managed, causing them to be fragmented or broken, as we will observe in the next chapter, and making it nearly impossible for entrepreneurs to negotiate the movement from one segment of the Pipeline to another.
- How long does it take entrepreneurs and enterprises to move to another segment of the Pipeline?
- What factors influence the probability of movement to another part of the Pipeline, the difficulty in doing so, and the risk of stagnation or failure?

The best way to evaluate the answers to these questions is by comparing the community's Pipeline performance to those of other communities or regions. We strongly suggest that a comparison be made both to regions of similar size and characteristics as well as to those with very different, but desired, characteristics. The advantage of benchmarking to very different locations is that it will expand the reference points through which a community views itself.

In order to properly compare the Pipeline performance of regions of different sizes, the Pipeline numbers should be scaled (controlled for size); that is, instead of utilizing raw numbers, ratios such as per capita figures should be used in each cell. These comparisons should enable communities to consider the following kinds of questions:

- Which communities have a higher percentage of entrepreneurs from their population in their Pipeline? What impact does this have on various measures of economic wealth in the community, for example, per capita income, savings, home ownership, and the like?
- How do these communities differ in terms of the distribution of entrepreneurs and enterprises among the various segments of the Pipeline? For example, whose Pipeline has larger employers in particular segments, and how does this fact impact the average wage and benefit levels in that community? What percentage of these employers are home grown vs. attracted branch plants? What are the differences in the local wealth-creating impacts between these two sets of firms, analyzed by segment of the Pipeline they occupy?
- What differences exist among communities in terms of their rate of flow in and out of the Pipeline as well as between various segments? Why, for example, is Community A's average flow rate 10 percent when the rate for competitive communities in its class is 20 percent? What accounts for the difference? What economic impacts does this have on wealth in both sets of communities?

INTRODUCING OTHER ELEMENTS OF THE PIPELINE

In addition to indicating the skill level of the entrepreneur and stage in the business life cycle, any single entity in the Pipeline can be coded with multiple pieces of information:

- Market or industry: the nature of the market or industry in which the entrepreneur and the enterprise is operating—for example, biotech, pharmaceuticals, plastics manufacturing, and so on.
- Type of business: for example, informal firm, artisan or craft operation, sole proprietorship, corporation, and so on.
- Business goals of the entrepreneur (necessity, life style, growth, etc.)
- Geographical location
- Age of the firm

- Gender of the entrepreneur
- Race or ethnicity or other demographic characteristics of the entrepreneur
- Number of years the entity has occupied a particular cell in the Pipeline
- Business performance, as measured (where data is available) by: sales revenue, number of employees, profitability, return on equity, return on assets, value added per employee, and so on.[4] Performance should be compared to other firms in the given cell of the Pipeline or to others in that industry occupying that cell of the Pipeline.

Each of these variables is unique and can vary independently. By distinguishing them in our framework, we can obtain a clearer understanding of their relationship to one another. Using these variables, we can also construct additional Pipelines to give us different "slices" or perspectives on the community's economy, as the following examples demonstrate.

A MARKET CLUSTER PIPELINE

The Pipeline can be used to create a very different perspective on the business assets in a community that belong to a particular market segment or industry (known as a cluster). By sorting members of a cluster into the appropriate pipeline segments, we can observe the structure of that cluster in a highly differentiated manner, as the hypothetical example in Figure 5.4 portrays.

We believe that this way of examining the entrepreneurial assets of a market cluster is very useful. First, it focuses on entrepreneurs and highlights their importance to the success of a cluster, as opposed to concentrating solely on the numerous public and private institutions in a cluster that, while important, are external to the businesses themselves. This emphasis is important, because as one researcher indicates, "the recent 'institutional turn' in economic geography is wont to give the impression that supportive institutions matter as much, if not more than, the firms at the heart of the innovation process. . . . It is not that these strategies are wrong to emphasize the role of supportive institutional networks, just that the latter cannot be a substitute for a local corporate sector."[5]

Second, it enables practitioners and policymakers to segment the cluster in a disaggregated way. There is an underlying assumption in

FIGURE 5.4.

Map of the Community's Pipeline of Entrepreneurs and Enterprises by Market Segment or Cluster Plastics – SIC 30

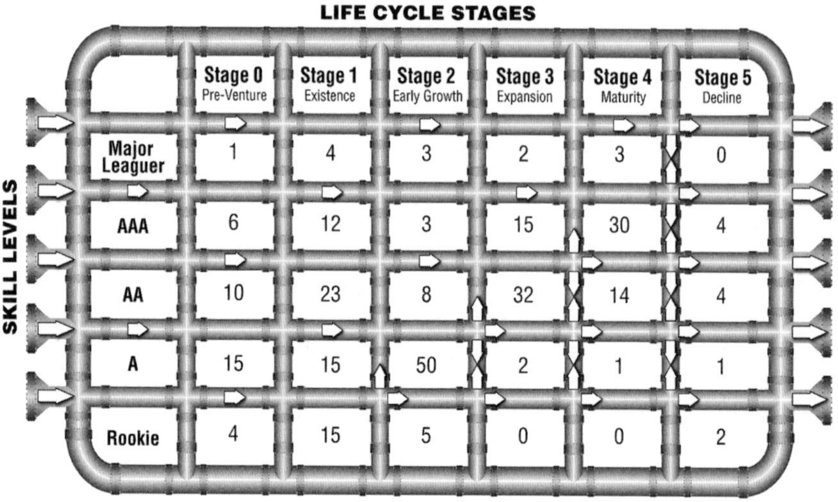

LIFE CYCLE STAGES

SKILL LEVELS

	Stage 0 Pre-Venture	Stage 1 Existence	Stage 2 Early Growth	Stage 3 Expansion	Stage 4 Maturity	Stage 5 Decline
Major Leaguer	1	4	3	2	3	0
AAA	6	12	3	15	30	4
AA	10	23	8	32	14	4
A	15	15	50	2	1	1
Rookie	4	15	5	0	0	2

this field that all businesses in a cluster have the same needs, and that service providers who focus on those needs will therefore be able to work with all of them. We believe this assumption is incorrect and that skill levels and life cycle stages are more important determinants of what firms need and how to work with them. Segmenting the members of a market cluster according to the pipeline allows entrepreneurship service organizations to provide much more sophisticated and targeted assistance to individual firms. The ideal arrangement would be for market cluster or industry specialists to partner with service providers who specialize in working with particular segments of the Pipeline and in this way address both issues.

GEOGRAPHIC PIPELINES

Each community's Pipeline of Entrepreneurs and Enterprises is unique. Because regional Pipelines are aggregates of the local Pipelines that comprise them, they tend to conceal the structural differences among the communities within their region. In order to get a better picture of the region's composition, we strongly suggest starting with the construction of local Pipelines, then putting these together to build a regional Pipeline.

For example, local Pipelines will reveal differences in the spatial distribution of firms. While a cluster analysis of the region's economy may indicate a concentration in secondary wood manufacturing, for example, a local Pipeline analysis would show how those firms are distributed among the communities. Therefore, any economic development strategy that is implemented for that cluster should take the geographical distribution into account.

We have long been advocates for what we have called distributed incubation programs. This means that each individual incubator in the group should specialize in a particular element of the Pipeline or particular market segment and serve the clients in the region that belong to that segment, no matter where they are physically located. Local Pipeline data would facilitate decisions not only about specific clientele to target in each community, but about the distribution of responsibility among incubators.

As this example illustrates, local Pipeline data would facilitate the development of strategic networks among entrepreneurs and enterprises throughout the region. Such initiatives could include targeted linkages between rural firms and urban markets, which would produce important economic benefits. The needs of distant or satellite communities in regions with powerful centers are often neglected. The development of local Pipelines could ensure that they receive attention and resources that are both strategic and commensurate with their economic contribution.

ASSET AGE PIPELINES

Another important take on the community's entrepreneurial assets involves examining the number of years that individual firms have occupied a particular segment of the Pipeline (this assumes we have access to historical data in this format). As economic developers, we would be concerned about the future viability of our economic base if we found that a large percentage of the entities in a particular segment have been there for a long time, say 10 or more years. This would be a red flag, suggesting that these entrepreneurs are experiencing difficulty in moving themselves and their businesses to another segment of the Pipeline.

This situation, particularly if combined with deteriorating financial performance in the form of downward pressure on pricing and margins or loss of market share, indicates stagnation rather than stability (which would be the case if firms are financially healthy). If entrepreneurs and their firms age without improving their ability to respond effectively to competitive conditions (by increasing their skill level for example), their continued viability is threatened.

Such entrepreneurs and their firms face extinction when economic or competitive conditions change quickly. We found this to be the case in our work with many inner-city manufacturers in Philadelphia, a large number of which had found a small market niche but had not changed their operations in any significant way for more than 30 years. We knew that this did not bode well, and those that continued on that course would soon fail with the passage of the North American Free Trade Agreement (NAFTA), which increased the use of contract manufacturers south of the U.S. border, and the growth in outsourcing to China.

Entrepreneurs in this situation are stuck. Either they can be targeted for support by economic development agencies, assuming that they are interested and willing to change, or they can be judged unviable. While the correct choice between these options can only be made after directly interacting with these entrepreneurs and making them an offer of support, the Pipeline data at least allow the economic developer to identify these entrepreneurs as a potential source of concern.

By indicating the ages of firms within each segment, we can generate yet another perspective on the Pipeline. This Pipeline data would help an economic developer to answer questions about the paths that businesses take through the Pipeline and the rate of speed of those journeys. It would enable the setting of more appropriate expectations and challenge myths or unreasonable assumptions, as did David Birch's finding, reported in chapter 4, that, in contrast to the belief that all gazelles (high-growth companies) are young, almost one-fifth have been in operation for 30 years or longer.

ECONOMIC PERFORMANCE PIPELINES

The economic performance of entrepreneurs and enterprises within specific Pipeline segments can be evaluated by collecting and analyzing additional data. One could sort all of the entities in a particular segment by percentile in terms of sales revenue generated, profitability (i.e., gross margins),[6] employment, value-added per employee, or various balance

FIGURE 5.5.
Distribution of Economic Performance of the Enterprises in a Particular Segment of the Community's Pipeline according to Revenue Generated

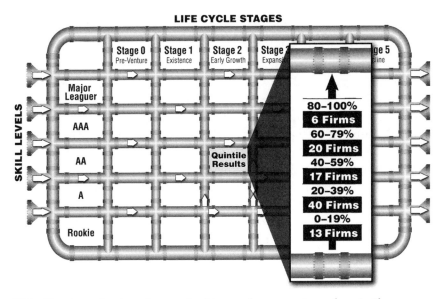

Note: Number of enterprises ranked by performance in each quintile as measured on the basis of revenue generated.

sheet items. (See Figure 5.5.) Bankers, for example, might be interested in determining how deposits or loan repayments differ by segments and within them. If Pipeline analysis were to become ubiquitous, comparisons could be made to national performance standards for each segment.

Economic developers could also compare the performance of each entity in a particular segment of the Pipeline against the performance of companies in the same industry from other communities also located in the same Pipeline segment. Another possibility is to index a company's performance against the average for its industry, and then rank the indices of those companies in a particular Pipeline segment, from high to low or on a percentile basis.

Each of these analyses represents a different way to assess the quality of the assets within a particular segment of the Pipeline, as measured by their financial performance. This information would enable economic developers to answer the following questions:

- What are the differences in performance across segments of the Pipeline? How does one explain these differences, if any?
- Are there any patterns?
- What factors influence the performance of firms in each segment of the Pipeline?
- How can we address these differences in performance (a subject to be examined in chapter 7)?

Clearly, there are many ways in which performance can be measured. It would be very useful to experiment with different measures to learn what they have to tell us. For example, when we have sufficient data in our project sites, we intend to examine the asset effects in each segment of the Pipeline, as well as the impact of Pipeline performance on social liabilities for particular demographic groups, such as the decrease in unemployment and welfare payments, or incarceration costs. This latter idea also suggests the possibility of additional Pipeline analyses in which entrepreneurs and enterprises are sorted on the basis of various demographic factors (e.g., gender or ethnicity) or type of business (e.g., informal firm, home business, artisan or craft operation, etc.).

ANALYZING A PIPELINE'S STRENGTHS AND WEAKNESSES

An economic developer should be asking the following questions subsequent to an assessment of his community's Pipeline:

1. How do you explain the differences in Pipeline performance between similar and different communities?
2. What are your community's goals or desired performance targets?
3. Given this particular description of your community's Pipeline, what are its strengths and weaknesses? What are the opportunities and threats?
4. What can be done to change the current Pipeline outcomes to be more favorable for the community or region?[7]

Communities or regions must realize that they are competing with other communities and regions, and that performance represents a competitive issue. While some regions are doing nothing or wondering what to do, others, particularly in other parts of the world, are taking action, which means relative performance is always changing, even if the status quo is being maintained.[8]

FIGURE 5.6.
The Pipeline Process

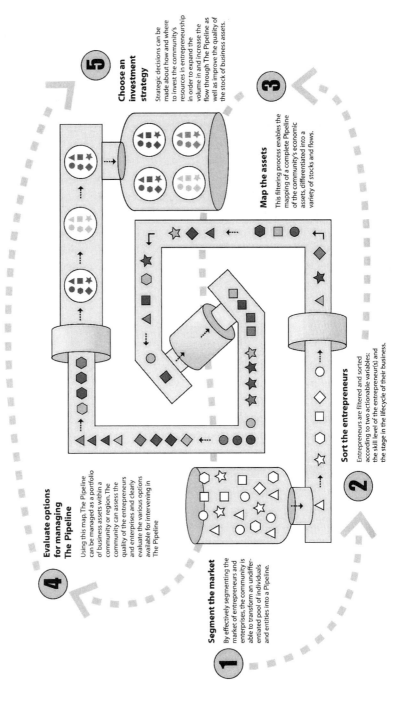

1 Segment the market

By effectively segmenting the market of entrepreneurs and enterprises, the community is able to transform an undifferentiated pool of individuals and entities into a Pipeline.

2 Sort the entrepreneurs

Entrepreneurs are filtered and sorted according to two actionable variables; the skill level of the entrepreneur(s) and the stage in the lifecycle of their business.

3 Map the assets

This filtering process enables the mapping of a complete Pipeline of the community's economic assets, differentiated into a variety of stocks and flows.

4 Evaluate options for managing The Pipeline

Using this map, The Pipeline can be managed as a portfolio of business assets within a community or region. The community can assess the quality of the entrepreneurs and enterprises and clearly evaluate the various options available for intervening in The Pipeline

5 Choose an investment strategy

Strategic decisions can be made about how and where to invest the community's resources in entrepreneurship in order to expand the volume in and increase the flow through The Pipeline as well as improve the quality of the stock of business assets.

WHAT A PIPELINE REPRESENTATION ALLOWS US TO DO

Pipelines, as maps, enable economic developers to represent the whole economy of a community or region and, at the same time, anatomize that whole into its constituent parts, so as to be able to see the relationship between the whole and its parts. The coding of the entrepreneurs and enterprises in the Pipeline, with pieces of additional information, gives us multidimensional views of the economy, instead of limiting the perspective to a single, fixed slice. One can go back and forth among these perspectives to begin to understand the relationship between these dimensions or can look at views within views (i.e., look at the impact of one variable on another). For example, one can analyze the differences in financial performance by market segments or look at how the age of the firms in a segment of the Pipeline varies by demographic characteristics. The Pipeline allows economic developers to be systemic as well as analytic. We will see in the next few chapters the power this gives us to better manage, and hopefully transform, our economies.

COMPARISON OVER TIME

No analysis can be complete without examining how the community's Pipeline changes over time. As economic developers collect longitudinal data in this format, the community will be able to see not only how these various dimensions of the economy relate to each other at a given point in time—a static presentation—but how they interact over time—a dynamic representation. In Chapter 6, we look at the dynamics within the Pipeline—in particular the relationship between the entrepreneur, the life cycle stages, and the market opportunity the entrepreneur is pursuing.

Diagramming the Pipeline Process

The diagram in Figure 5.6 charts the process by which individual entrepreneurs and enterprises are sorted into the appropriate segments in the Pipeline in order to produce a map of the community's assets. As will be seen in the following chapters, this then allows economic developers to evaluate various options for managing the Pipeline and then choose a specific investment strategy or strategies to achieve their goals.

6

Exploring the Dynamics within the Pipeline

Opportunity is missed by most people because it is dressed in overalls and looks like work.

—Thomas Edison

In chapter 3, we explained the ladder of skills and its importance to entrepreneurship. In chapter 4, we reviewed the six stages in the life cycle of a business. In chapter 5, we put these two dimensions together to form a Pipeline that enables a community to map its entrepreneurial assets. In this chapter, we explore the interrelationship between the two major elements that make up the Pipeline—entrepreneurial skills and the business life cycle—and examine the dynamics they produce.

These dynamics are created by the fact that skills and life cycle stages are separate variables, and that each can change independently of the other. This gives us 30 possible combinations (five skill levels multiplied by six life cycle stages), representing the number of cells in the Pipeline.

It is important to differentiate the business from the entrepreneur, because only in this way does it become possible to understand these dynamics. In the economic development field, people frequently attempt to sort businesses solely by the stage in their life cycle. As will be seen in this chapter, if the development process is reduced to one dimension, we are unable to explain the events we see every day.

OBSERVATIONS ABOUT THE PIPELINE OF ENTREPRENEURS AND ENTERPRISES

The Pipeline reflects the volume and flow of entrepreneurs and enterprises in the community or region. In order for the Pipeline to be sustained, there must be a continuous process of replenishment, with new entrepreneurs and enterprises replacing the old ones and small businesses growing larger and more mature.

There are a variety of possible outcomes for an entity in the Pipeline: movement to another segment of the Pipeline, stagnation/arrested development, performance improvement in a particular segment or attrition by death (e.g., bankruptcy or retirement). The Pipeline is dynamic; companies do not necessarily stay in a particular segment for long. External variables, such as market competition, heavily influence a firm's ability to stay in a particular segment. *Movement from one segment of the Pipeline to another requires a transformation—either the development of new skills or the evolution of the business to the next stage in the life cycle.*

In general, the distribution of skills in any community will resemble a pyramid—with fewer highly skilled people at the top and many low-skilled individuals at the bottom. This distribution exists in almost every field. Peers are, by definition, entrepreneurs at the same skill level, no matter what stage in the life cycle their business is operating. Role models are entrepreneurs who are at a higher skill level and/or whose business is at a later stage in its development.

The needs of entrepreneurs and enterprises in each segment of the Pipeline are different, as are the services and the infrastructure necessary to support them. This is a very important point. Entrepreneurship and innovation are issues in every part of the Pipeline; however, they take on very different forms in each segment.

The challenge in managing the Pipeline is how to increase both the quantity (i.e., volume) and the quality of the supply of entrepreneurs and enterprises in the community. The quality of the supply is a function of an entrepreneur's or enterprise's position in the Pipeline; it increases as they move to the upper right-hand corner—represented by the segments of higher skill level and later stages in the business life cycle. Within a given segment of the Pipeline, the higher-quality firms and entrepreneurs are those whose financial performance is superior to others in that segment, as well as others in their industry.

MAJOR PIPELINE CONDITIONS

There are several conditions, or states, in the Pipeline, generated by the interaction between skill level and the life cycle stage of the business: we call these Stable, Stuck, and Crash Points.

A Stable Point exists when there is balance between the skill level of an entrepreneur and the stage in the business life cycle, where the firm is performing well financially (within the limits prescribed by that segment of the Pipeline). An entity in the Pipeline could conceivably remain in this situation indefinitely; however, in reality, there are a number of forces that usually disturb this equilibrium: the entrepreneur's desire to move the business to the next stage in the life cycle or to increase his level of skill; an increase in market demand; or a decline in performance due to insufficient resources or competition.

For example, we have a client who is a Rookie with a successful plant brokerage business that she operates with a couple of part-time workers. She is making money and is very content. However, if market demand increases, she will be faced with a major problem: how to expand her capacity when she insists on doing all of the purchasing personally. To increase capacity, she would have to improve her skill level—to become a Single A and to learn, among other things, how to control the work by supervising others rather than performing it herself. Although she is currently operating at a Stable Point, her very success will likely produce the forces, such as growing market demand for her services, that will destabilize this equilibrium. So while her current state is a favorable one, it is in all likelihood a temporary condition.

STUCK POINTS

When performance declines, and neither the leader nor the business is advancing, the entrepreneur has reached a Stuck Point. There are particular segments in the Pipeline in which entrepreneurs tend to get stuck. For Rookies, it is at the Existence Stage in the life cycle; for Single As, it is at the Early Growth Stage (this is our operational definition of the so-called mom and pop shop, a huge logjam in the Pipeline), and for Double As, the Expansion Stage (see Figure 6.1). It is our experience that most of the community's business population will be found in these three Stuck Points.

How long entrepreneurs and their enterprises will be able to remain at a Stuck Point will be a function of competition. If competitive pressures are limited, entrepreneurs may be able to remain in that segment of the Pipeline indefinitely, even though it may be unproductive and unsatisfying to them. The purpose of preparing a Pipeline map exhibiting the length of time an entity has occupied the same segment (as

FIGURE 6.1.
Stuck Points in the Pipeline

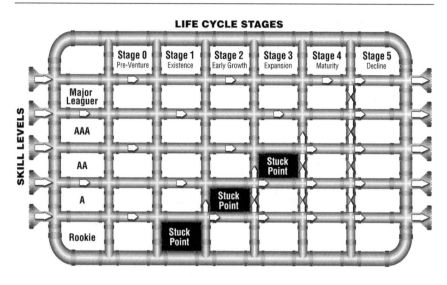

described in chapter 5) is to identify those entrepreneurs who have succumbed to this fate.

CRASH POINTS

A team of MBAs had a very ambitious plan: to become a restaurant management company with more than 100 properties under management. The problem was that none of them had ever operated a restaurant. Within three months of graduation from business school, they had contracts with three restaurants; within 12 months, eight more, and within 18 months, they were out of business.

Almost everyone has had the experience of going to a new 35-seat restaurant in their town that starts getting popular. The owner obtains financing to accommodate demand by doubling the size of his operation, and three months later, he is out of business. These endings are not just typical of small businesses. How many people have watched Krispie Kreme or Boston Chicken do the same thing? Or, to take an example from high-tech, who remembers the Osborne Computer Corporation, founded by Adam Osborne in 1980 to produce personal computers? It represents one of the most spectacular rises and falls in the industry. It went from nothing to the top of the mountain and back to nothing in just three years, after having raised more than $10 million in financing in one of the hottest deals of 1982. This scene is all too familiar to those who work with entrepreneurs. Just ask any banker. It gets replayed countless times in every industry, market, and location, and by companies of all sizes.

What happened? To successfully execute their business plan, the team of MBAs needed the combined entrepreneurial and management skills of at least a Double A or Triple A. Instead, they had the skills of a Rookie (someone with very limited business experience). It does not require much predictive power to see that as they added responsibilities and complexities to their operation (in terms of the number of restaurants), their weaknesses would be quickly exposed, and they were—it led them to bankruptcy. This same dynamic occurred with the small restaurant owner, Adam Osborne, and, we believe, the management teams at Krispie Kreme and Boston Chicken. Their businesses grew beyond their skill level and, as a result, they crashed.

There are stages in the life cycle to which the entrepreneur cannot advance the business successfully *unless* he increases his skill level. Otherwise, the business becomes unstable and blows up. It reaches a Crash Point.

This dynamic can be illustrated by using the Pipeline. Sales grew but the business could not effectively move to the next stage in the life cycle (to the right of its previous position in the Pipeline) without an equivalent increase in the skill level of the entrepreneur or his team. In other words, at their current skill level, the only place they could successfully navigate their growing business was "off a cliff."[1]

As can be seen in Figure 6.2, there are at least two and possibly three crash points in the Pipeline—for the Rookie entrepreneur, it would occur at the Early Growth stage in the business life cycle, for the Single A entrepreneur at the Expansion stage, and possibly for a Double A, at the Maturity stage.

Too often, people just assume that entrepreneurs have the necessary skills to move the business forward. But this is a very dangerous assumption. The level of an individual's entrepreneurial skills limits how far the business can successfully progress. When the business grows beyond that limit, the outcome is almost inevitable—unless the entrepreneur seeks help. But usually at that point, the business is on fire and burning fast.

FIGURE 6.2.
Crash Points in the Pipeline

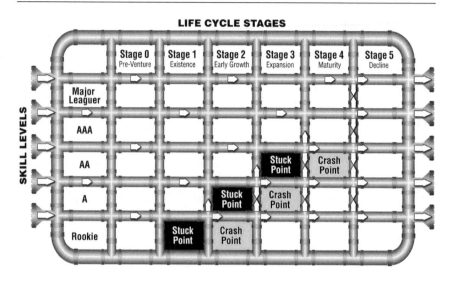

The lesson here is that entrepreneurial success requires a match between skill levels and the requirements of the business. The successful movement of the business to the next stage in the life cycle depends on the skills of the entrepreneur or her team. More highly skilled entrepreneurs will not only progress further through the stages in a business's life cycle, they will do so more quickly and with more efficiency than less skilled entrepreneurs.

OPTIONS

If this mismatch in skill level and life cycle stage is indeed a serious and an altogether too common scenario, what can be done to avoid it or reduce the costs in financial as well as human terms? What the team of MBAs should have done was to start with one restaurant, and when they had developed their ability to operate that business effectively (which might take a year or two), add another. Once they had mastered the skills to operate two, they could have added two or three more. Although the process of starting with this level of business activity and progressing to 100 restaurants under management may possibly have taken 10 to 12 years, the probabilities for success at each step of the way (or the ability to stop and exit gracefully without failure) would have been increased substantially. Instead, by going for the whole dream at once, all they did was to maximize their probability of failure. They were like Rookies stepping up to the plate for the first time ever in a Major League championship game and swinging for a home run.

At each step of the way, the team should have worked to increase their skill level *prior* to assuming more responsibility and greater complexity. By progressively increasing their skills and then matching their increased capacity with an increase in both the size and complexity of the business, they could have slowly but surely traversed the distance between their current reality and their highly ambitious business goals (see Figure 6.3 for the proper sequence of development moves through the Pipeline). It was doable, just not in a single step, nor in a compressed timeframe. The time and resources required to develop skills as well as to develop a business must be respected. A good coaching program, designed to develop entrepreneurial skills, would have facilitated this process.

In another example, an associate of ours who specializes in preparing business plans complained about the low rate of success among his

FIGURE 6.3.
Proper Sequence of Development Moves through the Pipeline

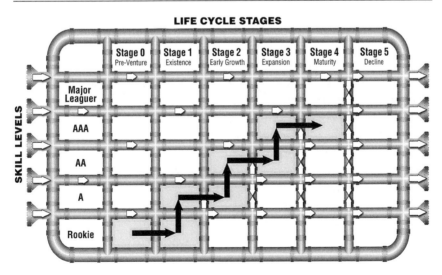

clients. He felt like he was capably preparing them for a journey to build a business, only to have them "die of thirst in the desert 40 miles from their starting point." He realized that the gap between their goals and their current reality was too vast to navigate, but who was he to discourage them from pursuing their dreams?

There are others who take the opposite position on this debate. They believe that people should be actively discouraged from pursuing a dream if it is clearly unrealistic. The Pipeline, however, enables us to see another view of this issue—a middle position that encourages entrepreneurs to pursue their dreams but at the same time insists that they be realistic about what it takes to achieve them.

The key is to manage the process of pursuing their dreams as a long-term journey, with discrete but multiple steps. Simply put, an entrepreneur must learn to crawl before she can walk and walk before she can run. The business that is created or operated at each step must be viable from a resource point of view, from a skills point of view, and from the market's point of view. Then, at each step in the journey, the probabilities of reaching one's ultimate goal hopefully become higher. It sounds very simple, but it is a rule that is frequently violated at great cost to the entrepreneur and to the economy as a whole. This is more than business planning; it is actually entrepreneurial career planning.

This rule of developing the necessary skill prior to assuming greater responsibility is an effective strategy, if the timeframe for developing skills fits within the window for capturing the market opportunity. In other words, the question is whether or not the entrepreneur has the time to develop on the job, or whether the market opportunity will be lost by the time that occurs. If the latter is the case, then the entrepreneur must consider other options.

One option is to add or change the management team in order to reach a higher skill level. The other is to sell or license the opportunity (not necessarily feasible unless it is more than an idea). Both options involve a loss of control, which is sometimes anathema to a less experienced entrepreneur. Although they do not necessarily see the situation in these stark terms, there are some entrepreneurs who would rather own 100 percent of an opportunity that earns nothing than 20 percent of a multimillion dollar business.

Personal maturity is required to make these judgments, as well as to successfully negotiate such deals, but it is the need to develop skills that is most difficult for less experienced entrepreneurs to understand. Instead, they are seduced by the thrill of the chase and the belief in popular but inaccurate myths about overnight entrepreneurial successes.

Even mature and successful businesses fail to understand the importance of entrepreneurial skills. One global telecommunications company with which we worked operated an internal venturing unit. We had been asked to assess the skill levels of two intrapreneurs leading very ambitious enterprises, for which the company had high expectations. Both were bright and highly motivated and possessed strong technical backgrounds. But one was a Rookie entrepreneur with no previous profit and loss experience, and the other was a low Single A. For a global company to be launching these ventures with intrapreneurs of such limited entrepreneurial skills was a low probability decision, in our opinion. Perhaps they could make it work, but the market window was not sufficient to permit them to learn on the job. It was a risky choice on the part of the company.

A small percentage of the total population of entrepreneurs can, and in many cases will, create many different businesses over the course of their individual lifetimes.[2] Often referred to as serial entrepreneurship, this pursuit of multiple businesses over time is a key to successfully building wealth. In contrast with corporations, it is impossible for an individual entrepreneur to diversify their risk by starting multiple businesses at one time. Instead, they launch what one entrepreneurship researcher calls "a temporal portfolio"—a portfolio through time.[3]

Like different seasons of a ballplayer's career, the journey of a serial entrepreneur consists of having many different businesses over their lifetime. While this stands in contrast with the entrepreneur who stays with one business throughout his career yet continues to develop both himself and the business, the path through the Pipeline is in many ways similar for both types.

Serial entrepreneurs develop their skills through a sequence of market opportunities or businesses, each appropriate to the skill level they occupy at that point in time. One serial entrepreneur told us that he pursued each business until it (or he) hit a "plateau" where he could develop it no further. He then sold it and used the proceeds to, in his words, "move sideways into another business opportunity" until he found another way to continue his upward progression. He explains that he is still following this pattern, even after having completed several cycles and having become extremely successful financially.

Using the Pipeline as a frame helps make sense of his experience. (See again Figure 6.3, which represents the proper sequence of development moves through the Pipeline. This figure captures the same pattern as the development path of a serial entrepreneur over time.) Starting out as a Rookie, he grew both his skills and his business but tapped out the potential of his business (a landscaping firm) when he reached the Single A level. In other words, he felt his business (not he himself as an entrepreneur) reached a plateau, and he could take it no further. He sold it and used his earnings to start another business that he felt had more economic potential (a restaurant) and presented a greater challenge to his skills as a Single A entrepreneur. Again, when he felt that he had reached the limit of that business's economic potential (he was probably now a Double A), he expanded his options as well as his business challenges by investing in a chain of restaurants and entering into local commercial real estate development. Today, now that he has reached what he believes to be the economic (or should we say, skill level) potential of this set of opportunities, he is again moving sideways in order to search for a new business that would give him the opportunity to grow even more, in terms of his skills as well as financial rewards.

The march of a serial entrepreneur through the Pipeline follows a pattern. That pattern includes starting a business, increasing one's skills, and achieving financial success; then, pursuing a more challenging business opportunity with larger economic potential that requires the further development of one's skills, followed by success and a continuation of the cycle. This example further illustrates the crucial separation of the business from the entrepreneur. Each individual business in this entrepreneur's temporal portfolio is the means by which he increases his skills and his wealth.[4] The businesses continue to exist as assets in the community or region even after he sells them to another entrepreneur.

THE FOUNDER'S DILEMMA

The Pipeline also helps us understand something known as the Founder's Dilemma. According to Noam Wasserman, a Harvard Business School professor who has researched this issue,[5] there is a trade-off in entrepreneurship between wealth and control. Most entrepreneurs want to make lots of money *and* run the show, but that is extremely difficult to do. Wasserman argues that entrepreneurs need to choose which value is more important to them; otherwise they could end up with neither. He asks us to consider the following scenario:

> To make a lot of money from a new venture, you need financial resources to capitalize on the opportunities before you. That means attracting investors—which requires relinquishing control as you give away equity and as investors alter your board's membership. To remain in charge of your business, you have to keep more equity. But that means fewer financial resources to fuel your venture. Startup founders who give up more equity to attract cofounders, key executives, and investors build more valuable companies than those who part with less equity. And the founder ends up with a more valuable slice of the pie. On the other hand, to attract investors and executives, you have to cede control of most decision making. And once you're no longer in control, your job as CEO is at risk. That's because: *You need broader skills—such as creating formal processes and developing specialized roles—to continue building your company than you did to start it* [emphasis added]. This stretches most founders' abilities beyond their limits, and investors may force you to step down.[6]

In another source Wasserman writes the following:

> More often than not . . . those superior returns come from replacing the founder with a professional CEO more experienced with the needs of a growing company. This fundamental tension requires founders to make "rich" versus "king" trade-offs to maximize either their wealth or their control over the company. Founders seeking to remain in control (as John Gabbert of the furniture retailer Room & Board has done) would do well to restrict themselves to businesses where large amounts of capital aren't required and where they already have the skills and contacts they need. *They may also want to wait until late in their careers, after they have developed broader management skills, before setting up shop* [emphasis added]. Entrepreneurs who focus on wealth, such as Jim Triandiflou, who founded Ockham Technologies, can make the leap sooner because they won't mind taking money from investors or depending on executives to manage their ventures. Such founders will often bring in new CEOs themselves and be more likely to work with their boards to develop new, post-succession roles for themselves.

Choosing between money and power allows entrepreneurs to come to grips with what success means to them. Founders who want to manage empires will not believe they are successes if they lose control, even if they end up rich. Conversely, founders who understand that their goal is to amass wealth will not view themselves as failures when they step down from the top job.[7]

As Wasserman explains, the way to avoid this dilemma is to select opportunities that do not require large amounts of capital (i.e., that are within one's means) and develop deeper skills, before taking on an opportunity of greater size and complexity. By pursuing a series of business opportunities over time that are progressively more sophisticated and resource-intensive, an entrepreneur may be able to achieve both wealth and control.

OTHER PIPELINE DYNAMICS

While it is tempting to do so, we have learned that *one cannot attribute skill level to an entrepreneur on the basis of the economic success of his or her business alone* (i.e., financial conditions do not always correlate with entrepreneurial skill). For example, we occasionally meet individuals who tell us that they must be a Triple A entrepreneur because they are millionaires.

One of the key factors in economic success of a business is the degree of competition in that industry or market. In the 1950s and 1960s, many towns in the United States had owners of hardware and office supply stores who were extremely successful financially. By using such success as one's indicator of skill level, it would be easy to conclude that they were high up on the skill level ladder. Most, however, were simply Single A entrepreneurs, who, when the big box stores (e.g., Home Depot, Lowes, Staples, and Office Depot) rolled into their communities in the 1980s and 1990s, simply could not compete and went out of business. Those stores that did survive and went on to thrive were owned by entrepreneurs who either were or developed themselves to be Double As. It would minimally require the skills of a Double A entrepreneur to compete successfully (usually on a niche market basis) with these global competitors.

As the economy becomes more and more competitive, a higher level of skill is required to achieve financial success than in the past. No longer are the skills of a Single A entrepreneur sufficient for success in highly competitive sectors. The bar continues to rise.[8]

Financial success can also be the result of luck. But unless the individual entrepreneur improves their skill, that result is never sustainable. We all know individuals who inherited a company (or married into one) whose "success" had little or nothing to do with their abilities and efforts. Under those conditions, the business inevitably fails.

INHERITING A FAMILY BUSINESS: WEAK POINTS

There are certain segments in the Pipeline that are theoretically unlikely to have any members: a Rookie at the Expansion stage, and a Rookie or Single A at the Maturity stage in the business life cycle. There are only two ways for this to occur—by inheriting the business or by buying it (remember that entrepreneurs can have money from other sources, also usually inherited, or from success in technical fields that did not require entrepreneurial skills). The probability of those ventures continuing to exist in the long run is extremely low. These Pipeline segments are known as Weak Points (see Figure 6.4).

Family businesses that are able to free themselves from this dynamic do so by relying on the development of entrepreneurial skill, not on luck. Either by drive or necessity, some individuals respond to luck by

FIGURE 6.4.
Weak Points in the Pipeline

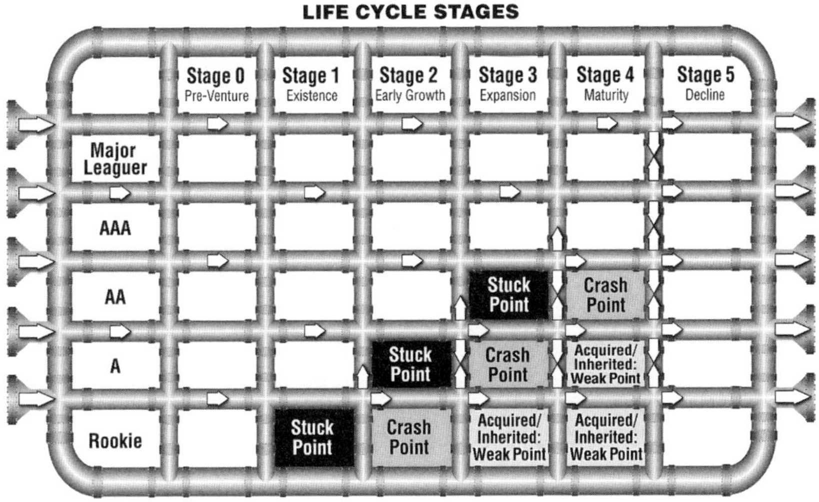

	LIFE CYCLE STAGES					
SKILL LEVELS	Stage 0 Pre-Venture	Stage 1 Existence	Stage 2 Early Growth	Stage 3 Expansion	Stage 4 Maturity	Stage 5 Decline
Major Leaguer						
AAA						
AA				Stuck Point	Crash Point	
A			Stuck Point	Crash Point	Acquired/ Inherited: Weak Point	
Rookie		Stuck Point	Crash Point	Acquired/ Inherited: Weak Point	Acquired/ Inherited: Weak Point	

developing their skills. In fact, the leaders of the more insightful family firms usually test the members of the next generation by making them get and succeed at a job in another business in order to demonstrate that they deserve to inherit the company.

We all know of situations where the second generation or later took the business to another level in terms of performance and financial success. To accomplish this result, they had to transform their business and themselves (move to a higher skill level and the next stage in the life cycle of the business; to a segment of the Pipeline higher and to the right of the cell they occupied when they inherited the business). They responded to the gift they received as an opportunity to progress.

Family businesses that last more than three generations are rare. This phenomenon is captured in the somewhat cynical but frequently accurate observation about the cycle of a family business: "Rags to rags in three generations." The first generation makes money (goes from rags to riches); the second generation holds or keeps the money; and the third generation squanders or loses the money (and so returns to rags).

FIGURE 6.5.
The Development Path of a Typical Family Business over Three Generations

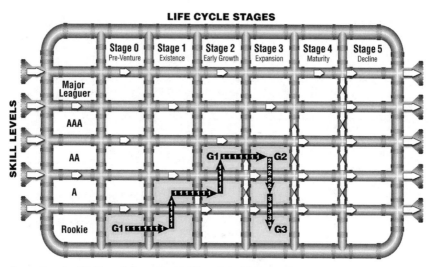

Generation 1 = G1 (Growth from Rookie/Stage 0 to AA/Stage 2)
Generation 2 = G2 (Stagnation from AA/Stage 3 to Single A)
Generation 3 = G3 (Collapse from Single A to Rookie)

We can actually trace this pattern in the Pipeline (see Figure 6.5). Usually the business is started by an entrepreneur who is or becomes a Double A and builds an enterprise of some scale. The son, who has grown up in the business and has had few experiences outside of it, is a Single A (or less) and maintains the status quo. The grandson is at best a Rookie who is unable to even maintain the status quo. The skill levels of the owners decline over the generations.

ONE-HIT WONDERS OR SERIAL ENTREPRENEURS

Then there are those entrepreneurs that are just plain lucky, who have the rare union of chance and a prepared mind. There is nothing wrong with that. Yet we have often encountered entrepreneurs who, as hard as they try, have a very difficult time repeating their success, even after a long string of attempts. How do we distinguish a serial entrepreneur from a one-hit wonder, someone who got lucky but didn't necessarily have the skills to do it again?

In our experience, one-hit wonders think that all they need to do to succeed in another business is to repeat what they did the first time. Sometimes, they don't really know what formula or combination of actions produced their initial success but are simply imitating their past behavior; sometimes they do, but fail to realize that that formula worked for a particular time and place that may not exist now or ever again. In other words, they don't understand that effective behavior is tied to a particular context or circumstances. Success has led them to believe that what they know will work in all situations. Because of this phenomenon, many people believe that human beings learn much more from their failures than from their successes. Failures force individuals to question what they know.

Significant success, particularly in an entrepreneur's first time out, can bias the thinking of others as well. Research suggests that "entrepreneurs who have attained superstar status may not only believe themselves to be more gifted than they actually are, but they may also draw investment and attention that they do not merit." As Starr and Bygrave argue, "success-seeking supporters are unlikely to impose discipline or offer constructive criticism, ironically rendering disappointment more likely."[9]

One-hit entrepreneurs will be unable to repeat their first performance over their career, unless their personal maturity gives them the desire and ability to overcome their limitations and develop new skills.

This is not to say that a serial entrepreneur will necessarily be success-ful in any or even all of their subsequent trials, but one would expect to observe a progressive change in skill as well as adaptations in their efforts to build each new business.

ENTREPRENEURIAL SPECIALIZATION BY STAGE IN THE LIFE CYCLE

Some entrepreneurs specialize in different stages in the business life cycle. For example, some individuals thrive best during the startup phases, which are more loosely structured, and prefer to exit the busi-ness as it becomes more formed (or in some cases, they need to be exited from the firm). For this specialization to be effective, the succession process must be formally managed.

TYPE OF BUSINESS DOES NOT NECESSARILY REFLECT THE ENTREPRENEUR'S SKILL

We have also learned that *one cannot infer the skill level of the entrepreneur on the basis of the business that they run.* The General Manager of our Ad-vantage Valley Entrepreneurial League System® coaching operation, who was responsible for recruiting clients, was a successful serial entrepre-neur, having launched and operated several technology ventures. His initial reaction, upon entering the premises of a commercial cleaning business, was to question what could possibly be innovative or entre-preneurial about such a low-tech firm. During his initial assessment, he found evidence of a bright and aggressive entrepreneur, increasingly successful, who was developing new products and working on plans to franchise his business. Not only did he come away impressed, but this event caused him to seriously reexamine his judgments about who is an entrepreneur and the sometimes unfair and inaccurate beliefs embed-ded within them.

We find these opinions to be common in economic development and business; we have been guilty of them ourselves but have learned to challenge the assumptions that drive them. The most important real-ization is that the entrepreneur is not identical with their business, and that one cannot conflate the two, nor assume that one can make judg-ments about one, simply on the basis of the other. One must look at both of them separately.

Nothing illustrates the arrogance of assuming an entrepreneur's skill from the nature of his business as effectively as the following true story of an immigrant from India. Shortly after arriving in the United States, this individual purchased a small convenience store, a common entry point for entrepreneurship among many south Asians. Several years later, having saved all he could from that business, he sold it and went into the import–export business. Three years later, he used the earnings from that business to obtain a patent for a software algorithm. Soon after, using this intellectual property, he launched what came to be a very successful high-tech business.

This entrepreneur had a Ph.D. in computer science as well as mathematics and came to this country with the idea for his business. What he did not have was the necessary financial resources (nor sufficient skills); at that time, the infrastructure to support high-tech Indian immigrants was not as developed in places like Silicon Valley as it is today. So his only choice was to leverage his limited resources and do it on his own. Through a sequence of business investments, each of which he grew to a point of maximum value to himself and then sold, he was able to fulfill his ultimate dream. The first two businesses served as intermediate steps to his eventual goal.

Anyone who would evaluate this individual's entrepreneurial skill on the basis of the kind of business he operates would miss seeing his current ability and his future potential. Using the business as an indicator of skill, while done regularly, reflects faulty thinking and results in errors of judgment. The business must be separated from the entrepreneur; only in that way can the dynamics between the two be understood.

In many cases, the wealth creation process starts with the pursuit of opportunities with low barriers to entry. Success and the acquisition of capital (as well as the increase in skills) gradually permit the pursuit of more costly, risky and, at the same time, more rewarding market opportunities in sequence.

It is difficult to make sense of the situations and stories presented in this chapter without reference to the Pipeline. Even more importantly, it becomes nearly impossible to do anything about them. When we present the Pipeline and tell these stories, community leaders, service providers, and entrepreneurs immediately recognize individuals and companies they know and place them in the proper segments. They also begin to see where entrepreneurs and businesses are stuck and what needs to be done to move them forward.

Many people in economic development and business ignore the skill dimension. In their view of the world, businesses move through their stages, apparently unaffected by the humans at their helm. They talk about businesses, jobs, and the like, but never about the entrepreneurs. The latter are simply not there. But without the entrepreneur, none of this would exist. We must learn to manage both the business and the entrepreneur as assets. Either alone is insufficient. In the next chapter, we will explore the economic development strategies needed to manage the Pipeline.

7

Strategies for Managing the Pipeline

I'm looking for a lot of men who have an infinite capacity to not know what can't be done.

—Henry Ford

Successful economic development requires effectively managing the flow and volume of entrepreneurs and enterprises in the Pipeline. This chapter examines the strategies or approaches that can be used to achieve this result. Economic development strategies can be sorted by their impact on the Pipeline. They fall into three broad categories:

1. Performance enhancement strategies designed to improve the quality of the assets or stock within each segment in the Pipeline—to increase or accelerate growth and profitability
2. Incubation strategies designed to change (i.e., transform) assets or stock by improving the flow or movement of entrepreneurs and enterprises between segments in the Pipeline
3. Selective attraction strategies designed to add new players or stock to the Pipeline

In the next section, we review each strategy and examine its strengths and weaknesses as well as the conditions under which it can be appropriately employed.[1]

PERFORMANCE ENHANCEMENT STRATEGIES

Performance enhancement strategies focus on improving business outcomes (i.e., growth in revenue, jobs, and profitability) for entrepreneurs and their enterprises that are operating within a particular segment in the Pipeline. When applying these strategies, the structure of the business and the skills of the entrepreneur are left unchanged; in other words, the entrepreneur and the enterprise remain in the same segment of the Pipeline, although at a more profitable level of operation and/or a larger size. The changes that results are only quantitative, not qualitative, in nature. We liken performance enhancement strategies in economic development to putting an athlete on steroids. This does not enhance the athlete's skills, nor does it change her basic body structure. It merely "pumps up" her performance (see Figure 7.1).

The following is a list of various approaches for enhancing business performance:

- Profitability improvement or cost reduction strategies
- Sales or market growth strategies
- Operational improvement efforts or refinements
- Adoption of best practices
- New hires—for example, exiting out the founder, changing management players, but keeping the existing structure in place

FIGURE 7.1.

Managing the Pipeline Using Performance Enhancement Strategies

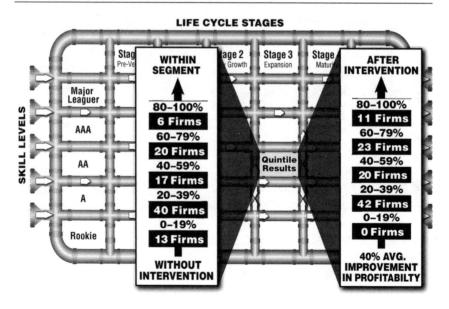

- Workout programs—for example, General Electric's program[2]
- Turnaround consulting efforts—emergency or crisis efforts
- Asset sale—that is, of the business or any component—for financial, not strategic purposes[3]

The strength of performance enhancement strategies is that they can produce results relatively quickly—they accelerate the process—when focused, for example, on firms that are ready to grow their sales by at least a few million dollars within a year. However, their impact is limited to the number of firms (i.e., the quantity or stock) already in that segment of the Pipeline, because this approach is not capable of moving firms from one location in the Pipeline to another (something that requires a transformation). Once those firms participate, there is no way, using this strategy, to generate new clients. Thus, the weakness of this strategy is its lack of operational sustainability over the long term (i.e., once the cream is gone, who is responsible for making more cream?).

For performance enhancement strategies to be effective, clients must already be primed—that is, they have to be ready, willing, and able (in terms of their skills) to take action and make use of the technical and financial assistance being provided to quickly achieve results. In order to speed up the process by which enterprises get ready for venture funding, these initiatives must focus on enterprises that have already completed their Pre-Venture stage of development and on entrepreneurs that already have a high level of skill. In order to achieve substantial increases in sales, jobs, and profits in a relatively short period of time, it is necessary to focus on later stage businesses—usually those at or ready to enter stage 3 (Expansion or Sustained Growth). In the desire for quick results, performance enhancement strategies must take a very narrow cut from the Pipeline—meaning, selecting the low-hanging fruit.

When resources alone are sufficient to produce a significant increase in performance, it is an indication that a transaction involving the delivery of technical and financial assistance is necessary. When changes in capacity of the entrepreneur and the enterprise are required, it indicates that a transformation is necessary. In these latter cases, we must look to incubation strategies in order to successfully intervene in the Pipeline.

INCUBATION STRATEGIES

Incubation strategies are designed to change (i.e., transform) the assets or stock by improving the flow or movement of entrepreneurs and

FIGURE 7.2.
Managing the Pipeline Using Incubation Strategies

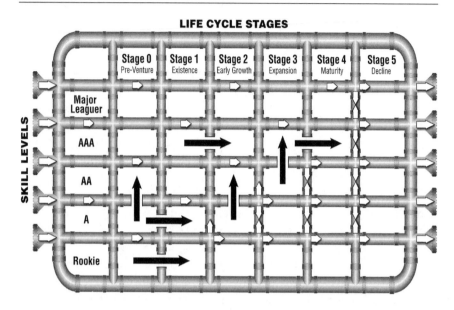

enterprises between segments in the Pipeline. In this set of strategies, the current structure of the business and the current skill level of the entrepreneur (and/or his or her team) is not taken as a given—it is the focus of the change efforts. Incubation strategies produce qualitative as well as quantitative changes in the enterprise and the entrepreneur (see Figure 7.2).

The following strategies can be used to incubate various segments of the entrepreneurial Pipeline:

- Develop the skills of entrepreneurs
- Build, change, or add to the management team—to bring in higher levels of skills[4]
- Change ownership or control—for example, through the sale of the business (through business brokering); succession planning;[5] exiting out the entrepreneur, or transferring them to a different opportunity better suited to their skill level
- Recruit new talent—for example, youth entrepreneurship and the like
- Launch intrapreneurial ventures (corporate venturing) or develop new products (not merely line extensions) within mature companies

- Spin out new, independent ventures from larger, mature firms
- Transition enterprises to the next stage of development in the business life cycle
- Reinvent stagnant firms

The strength of incubation strategies lies in the fact that they are sustainable over the long term. They are an approach for building the Pipeline, not just improving the performance of certain parts of the Pipeline. The challenge is that these strategies require skill to execute as well as a significant investment of time and resources.

SELECTIVE ATTRACTION STRATEGIES

Selective attraction strategies are designed to add new players (i.e., stock) to the Pipeline in a highly targeted way. The goal is to recruit entrepreneurs and companies to the community whose capabilities complement those of existing firms, and who, as a result, will provide significant leverage to other firms in capturing market opportunities or in enhancing the performance of these existing firms. A simple example would be the effort to attract a finishing business to a community with a number of furniture manufacturers already operating there who currently must send their products out of the community to be finished or who must sell unfinished furniture and receive a lower price for the sale of a lower-value-added product.

The difference between this strategy and traditional business attraction initiatives is that selective attraction strategies are specifically pursued for the purpose of changing the composition of the business assets in the community (the stock in the Pipeline), not simply in order to increase the number of entrepreneurial assets (i.e., a change in size). This change in composition produces benefits for more than just the individual business that has been recruited. It is this leverage and the impact on other firms that differentiates this approach from traditional attraction strategies (see Figure 7.3).

Examples of selective attraction strategies include:

- Recruiting aspiring entrepreneurs or actual entrepreneurs and their businesses—for example, encouraging immigration
- Mergers and acquisitions by mature companies within the community
- Strategic business attraction or relocation

FIGURE 7.3.

Managing the Pipeline Using Selective Attraction Strategies

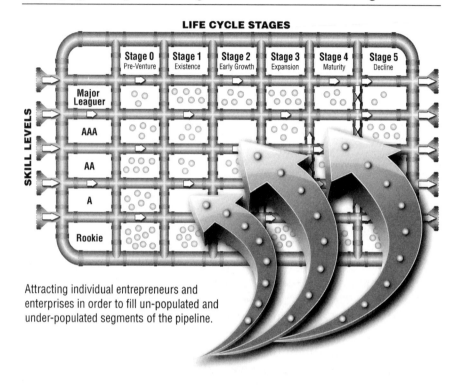

Attracting individual entrepreneurs and enterprises in order to fill un-populated and under-populated segments of the pipeline.

- Encouraging the establishment of satellite operations or "branch plants" by a larger organization
- Franchising[6]

On the surface, these examples look no different than those traditionally pursued. Again, the difference is in how the strategy is executed. For example, franchises that are attracted for the purpose of generically adding to the stock of entrepreneurial assets in the community would not be consistent with this approach.

Selective attraction strategies are much more challenging to execute successfully than traditional attraction strategies. Economic developers must possess a far deeper knowledge of their local business capabilities, and a broad vision about what businesses would complement them. This may make it a difficult strategy for existing staff to execute.

For this reason, it should not be left solely to professional economic development staff but must involve active participation by the business community. If successful, however, this strategy produces synergies, brings the community capabilities that did not exist before, and helps root the new firm in the community through its relationships with other companies.

Selective attraction strategies can also serve a development function, by focusing on recruiting entrepreneurs who can serve as role models to other entrepreneurs in the Pipeline. As noted in the sidebar in Chapter 3 on Categorizing Entrepreneurs According to their Goals, an entrepreneur's choice of goals is heavily influenced by the kind of entrepreneurs to which he has been exposed in his life. If a community identifies a lack of appropriate role models in certain segments of the Pipeline as an impediment to other entrepreneurs, it would be well served to target those entrepreneurs for attraction.[7]

OBSERVATIONS ABOUT ECONOMIC DEVELOPMENT STRATEGIES

These three sets of strategies for managing the Pipeline of Entrepreneurs and Enterprises—performance enhancement, incubation and selective attraction— can be used in every segment of the Pipeline. This fact is not clearly understood, particularly with regard to incubation of entrepreneurship strategies. There is a tendency to identify entrepreneurship only with startups, especially new, independent company formations, and to believe that entrepreneurship is not relevant at other stages in the business life cycle. This thinking contributes to the artificial bifurcation, in both the research literature and in practice, between independent entrepreneurship and entrepreneurship within existing companies (also known as intrapreneurship). While each occurs in a different context, there is a great deal of functional similarity; much that applies to entrepreneurs can be used to assist intrapreneurs as well.

There are three main methods of impacting the quantity and quality of the assets in the community's portfolio:

- Increase the volume—the number or quantity—of entrepreneurs and enterprises in the Pipeline as a whole or in particular segments.
- Increase the flow through the Pipeline.
- Increase the quality (i.e., the performance) of the assets within a particular segment of the Pipeline.

Throughout this book, we have stressed the difference between growth and development, and the need to focus on development. The Pipeline illustrations in this chapter (i.e., Figures 7.1, 7.2, and 7.3) make the difference between growth and development very clear. Performance enhancement and strategic attraction are strategies for growth, not development. Selective attraction has to do with increasing the volume within a segment of the Pipeline, and performance enhancement has to do with increasing the size and profitability of the assets within a segment. *Only incubation strategies produce development—by increasing the flow from one segment in the Pipeline to another.* In order to transform our economies and successfully put development back into the field of economic development, we need to emphasize incubation strategies.

The choice of a strategy is a function of what one wants to accomplish. If for example, the goal is to increase the flow of entrepreneurs and enterprises from the Single A, Early Growth Stage to the Double A, Expansion Stage, from its current annual rate of 5 percent to 20 percent, an initiative from the set of incubation strategies would be appropriate. If the goal is to increase the profitability as well as the asset value of Double A firms at the Mature Stage, this would call for certain approaches from the category of Performance Enhancement strategies. These examples demonstrate how the Pipeline can be used to provide a concrete basis for making *strategic* decisions about where to invest limited resources in the community's portfolio of entrepreneurial assets.

In order to be effective, economic development strategies must be targeted to a specific part of the Pipeline. This is because the needs of an entrepreneur or enterprise in each cell of the Pipeline are different. Any initiative that is not tailored to a particular segment runs the risk of being ineffective with all of its clients. This statement merely recognizes that no individual program, person, or company is capable of doing more than one thing well, at the same time, particularly if those activities are very different and require exercising vastly different capabilities. This is not a failing; it is a fact of life. The failure would be in refusing to accept this reality, by attempting to be all things to all people and, as a result, having little or no impact on anyone.

When it chose to enter the luxury car market, Toyota had to create an entirely separate business, brand, and identity. It could not do so with a venture that at that time was known for low-end, high-quality vehicles. Toyota needed different people, different operations, and different marketing messages. It could only specialize by launching an independent entity and letting it operate according to a different set of rules. IBM, too, understood this principle when it launched its personal computer division in the early 1980s and located it in Florida, far away from the corporate headquarters.

We strongly believe that the failure to effectively target (and to be disciplined about maintaining that target) is the reason why economic development initiatives don't have more impact. We are calling for specialization in our economic development strategies. Most organizations are good at something—usually one thing—and that is what they should focus their resources on. Coverage of the various needs in different parts of the Pipeline should come from a system of specialist organizations or initiatives that are linked together, not from the attempt by a single organization to cover all of the bases.

For this reason, we are generally skeptical of the impact of general-purpose incubators. It is not the variation in client business types that is the problem; it is the fact that they are trying to serve clients in various segments of the Pipeline. Incubation can be employed in any segment of the Pipeline, but for a particular application to be successful the target population must be specified. Being client-centered means using the Pipeline to differentiate the community's population of entrepreneurs and enterprises, targeting a particular segment and then implementing an economic development strategy to achieve the desired results.

Targeting Service Providers by Pipeline Segment

Service providers from the private, public, and nonprofit sectors who work with entrepreneurs and their businesses can be sorted by the segment of the Pipeline in which they tend to specialize, intentionally or without knowing it. Figure 7.4 is an illustration drawn from our experience.[8] In it, we make some broad generalizations. One of the problems that exists in many regions is that rarely do formal or even informal ties exist among these providers. As a result, it is difficult for entrepreneurs to smoothly transition from one to another as needed. Coordination among providers is needed to achieve the objective of ensuring that an entrepreneur gets the right help at the right time in her individual development and that of her company.

FIGURE 7.4.

Illustration of Pipeline Segments Typically Targeted by Economic Development Service Providers

Skill Level:	Stage 0 Pre-Venture	Stage 1 Existence	Stage 2 Early Growth	Stage 3 Expansion	Stage 4 Maturity	Stage 5 Decline
Major Leaguer		V.C.'s, professional consulting practices, investment bankers, etc.				Turnaround Specialists
AAA	Angel Investors, University Tech Transfer	V.C., Emerging Business Consulting Practices	V.C., Emerging Business Consulting Practices	V.C., Emerging Business Consulting Practices	Private Equity	Investment Banks, Turnaround Specialists
AA		Technology Business Incubators, Private Consultants	Technology Business Incubators, Private Consultants	Manufacturing Extension, Private Consultants	Manufacturing Extension, Private Consultants	Turnaround Specialists, Business Brokers
A	SBDC's	SBDC's, Business Incubators, Fastrack Business Planning	SBDC's, Business Incubators	Manufacturing Extension	Manufacturing Extension	Business Brokers
Rookie	Youth Entrepreneurship	Micro-enterprise programs				

Note: Other programs or initiatives that could be included in the table in this figure are: SCORE, community revolving loan funds, other gap financing providers, mezzanine financing, banks, regulatory streamlining and information programs, tax incentives/abatement programs, and enterprise zones or empowerment zones.

EVALUATING PIPELINE STRATEGIES

While the number and variety of strategies for encouraging entrepreneurship continue to proliferate, no one seems to know how to evaluate their effectiveness and, on the basis of that knowledge, strategically choose from among them in order to achieve community economic goals. Questions abound:

- Are economic development programs working? How do we know?
- How do community business leaders, economic developers, and government officials choose where to invest their scarce resources?
- What kind of value are we getting for our investment?
- How do these returns compare to alternative uses of the same funds?

The simple fact of the matter is that, in most cases, we don't know. We have almost no knowledge of what works, under what conditions, and how well. Because such knowledge is lacking, decision makers do not have the information they need to make good choices. Should we continue to fund Program X, expand it, or close it down? Do we need another similar program, serving a different clientele, or should we consider an entirely new approach? Is it wise to concentrate on supporting startup companies that have high-growth potential or to adopt a more broad-based approach? In the end, it seems that most decisions about economic development programs are made on the basis of politics,[9] personality, subjective preference, or fads. This manner of operating is unacceptable from a community standpoint; yet, no one seems to know how to change it.

The problem is not merely an absence of data; it is an absence of knowledge. For example, the data from an industry study of business incubation tell us that the average tenure of a business in an incubator is 2.5 years.[10] But what does that mean? Is that good or bad? Is it too short— are we prematurely pushing businesses out before they are ready? Or is it too long—are we providing far more support than is necessary? To have or produce knowledge, we must understand the context or conditions under which we are working and have a framework by which to evaluate the data.

To more effectively professionalize the field of economic development, we must create a foundation for making decisions among various options that is grounded in reality—the reality of the marketplace of entrepreneurs in our communities and regions. We need a better framework for evaluating strategic options. In this section, we discuss five evaluation criteria for judging economic development strategies and their impact on the Pipeline.

In making evaluations of almost any kind, there are three major sources of conflict among individuals (and organizations), about which they are frequently unaware:

- Differences in what is being examined (i.e., the object)—in this case, the variety of options for managing the community's Pipeline of Entrepreneurs and Enterprises
- Differences in the perspective from which, and criteria by which, people judge a particular "object"
- Differences in the particular valuation or judgment placed on the object—even when it is the identical object being viewed from the same perspective and with the same evaluation criteria

By recognizing these sources of conflict, we can clarify the confusions that frequently arise in evaluations of economic development strategies, identify the real and vital differences, and manage those differences in order to achieve better outcomes.

In the previous section, we articulated the "what" of economic development—the various strategies for managing the Pipeline of Entrepreneurs and Enterprises. In this section, we look at the differences in perspectives and criteria by which these individual strategies can be evaluated. We need to evaluate management decisions so that we can establish that the correct choices are being made.

As we have argued elsewhere,[11] if we are being comprehensive, options for managing the Pipeline should be evaluated in terms of five different criteria:

1. Effectiveness
3. Equity
4. Sustainability
2. Efficiency
5. Scale of impact

The Effectiveness Criterion

There are four desired outcomes for the effectiveness of various options for intervening in the Pipeline. Each of these outcomes is, conceptually and with the proper resources, measurable. Data on these measures would enable informed judgments of the effectiveness of various strategies. The following is a list of measurement variables by type of desired outcome:

1. The increase in the rate of business formation over time:

   - The expansion in the number of entrepreneurs within the community
   - The expansion in the number of new enterprises launched within the community
   - The number and breadth of the settings from which entrepreneurs are drawn (e.g., geographical areas and various populations), and in which enterprises are launched (e.g., within existing firms and between firms)
   - The capture of market opportunities within the community that would otherwise be lost
   - The number of matches made between market opportunities and entrepreneurs who want to start a business but have no business concept

2. The increase in the rate of survival and success of enterprises:

   - The increase in the overall survival and success rate of enterprises within the community
   - The increase in the probability of success for particular enterprises
   - The reduction in the length of the time required to achieve success (at different stages of development of the business)
   - The reduction in the cost of launching and/or operating a business
   - The increase in the value of the business assets in the community and the wealth generated

3. The increase in the rate of development of entrepreneurs and their enterprises:

   - The changes (and rate of change) in the skill levels of entrepreneurs
   - The changes (and rate of change) in the stages of development of the business

   These two variables, in particular, give us a concrete means of measuring development as opposed to growth and are an indication of the effectiveness of the development process

4. The increase in the effectiveness of the dissolution process if a firm fails (changes in the speed at which human and physical resources are recycled into the economy).

Because failure is an integral part of entrepreneurship, the speed with which these assets, including the entrepreneur, return to other economically productive uses is very important. Unfortunately, we have observed that regions with low rates of entrepreneurship are usually those where entrepreneurs experience a great deal of negative feedback about failure, often resulting in considerable shame, in contrast with regions with high rates of entrepreneurship. It is said that venture capitalists in places like Silicon Valley impartially evaluate both failures and successes as an important element of the entrepreneur's track record, knowing that you don't have one without the other.

One entrepreneur with whom we worked told us that it took him over five years to raise money in his community (which was not known for its enterprising nature) for his next venture, after his first had failed. Using lessons he had learned from that failure, his new venture has been doing well. Although there are several ways to look at this issue, the question we're asking here is what opportunities and benefits were lost on both a personal and a societal basis by the time delay he experienced in getting back into the game.

The Efficiency Criterion

Efficiency is a measure of the difference in the value of the benefits produced by these outcomes in the Pipeline (both monetary and nonmonetary) over time[12] and the level of resources required to achieve them (i.e., the return on investment).[13] It is important that the calculations be as comprehensive as possible in capturing benefits. Typical calculations include dollars invested per job created, increase in sales over dollars invested, and so on.

The Equity Criterion

Equity is a measure of the distribution of benefits and costs to various members of the community from different options for managing the Pipeline. Equity issues are fairly complex to address. In order to evaluate them accurately, one must first trace the benefits and costs. Then one is in a position, on the basis of confirmable data, to make judgments about the equity of particular distributions of benefits and costs.

Particular distributions must be looked at both from the perspective of the various individual community members or stakeholder groups and from the perspective of the community as a whole. For example, there is research that suggests that regions with a more narrow income distribution perform better economically.[14] Any approach used to evaluate equity should enable us to answer the following questions:

- What are the total benefits of these outcomes (as described by the following dimensions)?

  - Direct and indirect
  - Private versus public
  - Positive and negative externalities (or "system" returns made possible only by the existence of a "whole")
  - Tangible and intangible (e.g., learning from failure, etc.)

- How are these benefits distributed within the community, that is, who in the community (which community members), specifically, are capturing the benefits from these outcomes? Are the benefits inclusive? Why or why not?
- What is the monetary value of these benefits (if it is possible to calculate)?
- Who is incurring the costs of these strategies?
- To what extent are the community members who are receiving the benefits contributing to the production of these benefits? What are these stakeholders able to contribute to the production of these benefits?

The Sustainability Criterion

The question of the sustainability of various investments in the Pipeline can be divided into four dimensions:

- Operational sustainability: how long can the particular strategy be feasibly continued? Is there a limit, and if so, what is it?
- Financial sustainability: how long can the community afford to engage in this strategy?
- Environmental sustainability: how does this strategy (or the output of the firms affected by the strategy) impact the community's environment or ecosystem?[15]

- Economic sustainability: how does the strategy impact the community's economy and its Pipeline?

The Scale of Impact Criterion

Pipeline strategies must also be evaluated on the basis of their scale of impact on the community's economy. Possible measures include:

- The number of entrepreneurs included or participating as a percentage of the total number of entrepreneurs in the community
- The number of enterprises included or participating as a percentage of total businesses or ventures in the community

STANDARDS FOR COMPARING PERFORMANCE

There are various standards against which to compare the performance of options for managing the Pipeline on each of these criteria.[16]

- Past performance
- Desired outcomes
- Other locations with similar geographic or demographic characteristics
- Capability, defined as what the community could be doing right now with existing resources under existing constraints
- Potential, defined as what the community ought to be doing by developing its resources and removing constraints, although still operating within the bounds of what is already known to be feasible
- Creation of new potential, defined as what can be done to change the bounds of what is feasible (i.e., through innovation and the creation of entirely new possibilities)
- Alternative investment opportunities

The nature of the conclusions that can be drawn depends on the standard that is selected for comparison. This choice must be intentionally made (not simply on the basis of what kind of data is available) and clearly articulated. One of the challenges is to design strategic options for managing the Pipeline that have a positive impact on as many of these five evaluation criteria as possible (see Table 7.1).

TABLE 7.1.
Summary of Evaluation Criteria for Economic Development Strategies and their Impact on the Pipeline

1. EFFECTIVENESS

   a. **Increase in the rate of business formation over time:**
- Number of new entrepreneurs
- Number of new enterprises
- Number of settings from which entrepreneurs are drawn
- Number of market opportunities captured
- Number of matches made between market opportunities and entrepreneurs

   b. **Increase in the rate of survival and success of enterprises:**
- Enterprise survival and success rate
- The increase in enterprise probability of success
- The reduction in the length of the time required to achieve success
- The reduction in the cost of launching and/or operating a business
- The increase in the value of the business assets

   c. **Increase in the rate of development of entrepreneurs and their enterprises:**
- The changes (and rate of change) in the skill levels of entrepreneurs
- The changes (and rate of change) in the stages of development of the business

   d. **The increase in the effectiveness of the dissolution process if a firm fails**

2. EFFICIENCY
- Benefits compared to costs over time

3. EQUITY
- Total benefits
- How benefits are distributed
- Monetary value of these benefits
- Who is incurring the costs
- Are costs and benefits matched

4. SUSTAINABILITY
- Operational sustainability
- Financial sustainability
- Environmental sustainability
- Economic sustainability

5. SCALE OF IMPACT
- The number of participants as percentage of total entrepreneurs
- The number of enterprises as percentage of total businesses

HOW TO CHOOSE A PIPELINE STRATEGY

How does a community evaluate particular strategies for use? In theory, the marketplace of ideas has provided communities with dozens of contenders for the status of "holy grail" of enterprise development—clusters, the creative class, venture capital, enterprise facilitation, and so on. In reality, such claims are questionable, because in practice there is no single strategy that will be right in every case; in other words, the best choice, or choices, very much depends on the unique conditions in each community. In order to build systemic solutions, each community must create a unique recipe whose elements consist of many of these strategies, in a planned combination. The Pipeline permits economic developers to develop synergistic policies and programs that will enhance the flow and volume of their entrepreneurs and enterprises. In the next chapter, we explore how these strategies, and their accompanying tactics, can be employed to address challenges in various areas of the Pipeline.

8

Using the Pipeline
to Design Strategic Options

We chose to go to the moon in this decade and do the other things, not because they are easy, but because they are hard, because that goal will serve to organize and measure the best of our skills and talents, because that challenge is one we are willing to accept, one we are unwilling to postpone and one we intend to win, and the others, too.

—President John F. Kennedy, Address at Rice
University, Houston, Texas, September 1962

Eleven critical economic challenges that confront many regions throughout the world are laid out in this chapter. We then analyze each situation using the Pipeline as our diagnostic framework. We will describe the traditional approaches to these challenges and compare them to different strategic options that the Pipeline analysis helps reveal. Finally, we present an example of how to design these strategic options in order to hit their targets and achieve a measurable return-on-investment.

SCENARIO 1: BUSINESS CLOSURES
DUE TO SUCCESSION ISSUES

Communities across the country have viable businesses that are closing for lack of someone to take over the business when the owner retires.[1] Not only is the owner unable to sell the business for a financial return, communities are losing a valuable economic asset. This is happening in a number of highly skilled professions such as the building trades (e.g., plumbing, electrical contracting, etc.), as well as in manufacturing sectors such as machine tooling. It is a growing problem in the agricultural sector as well.

We must develop successful strategies for wealth preservation in succession situations and at the Decline Stage in the Pipeline. Suggestions for strategic options include referring owners to business brokers, and convening seminars on succession or tax and estate planning. But in most communities, nothing is being done to address this issue; perhaps because it is being seen as beyond the responsibility of any enterprise assistance organization. As a result, valuable opportunities are being lost.

Not only are these suggestions rarely being implemented, they only deal with one of three aspects of the problem: the supply of available businesses. They fail to do anything about identifying prospective entrepreneurs who might be interested in purchasing those businesses, or the process of making a successful match between the two parties.

Every community has individuals that want to start or own a business. These individuals need to be made aware of and directed to opportunities to purchase existing businesses. That means information about these opportunities must be collected and made available to potential prospects in a methodical way. Because of the sometimes sensitive nature of business sales, this must be done with care. There are ways to use the Internet to facilitate these connections on a double-blind basis or to utilize local business brokers.

While awareness of the availability of a business for sale is an important condition, it is far from sufficient to insure that a sale is made. We believe that the limited success of business brokering is due to the uncertainty and risk on both the seller's and buyer's side. Sellers are reluctant to accept payments over time, for example, because they are uncertain about the buyer's ability to succeed in the business (i.e., uncertain about their entrepreneurial skills). Such payment plans are often the only way many buyers can afford to acquire a business even with financing; so, if this avenue is blocked because of such uncertainty, many potential deals will not be consummated. By organizing the market for entrepreneurs and establishing a credible way of assessing skills, such business brokering could be made much more effective.

The proper assessment of entrepreneurial skills is critical.[2] It must be determined whether or not the prospective entrepreneur has the right skills to deal with the situation that the business is in as it is being sold. We have observed laid-off executives, with funds from their employment buy-outs, purchase businesses in industries with which they were familiar. However, many of these businesses were in the Decline Stage and needed to be reinvented. This situation calls for significant entrepreneurial skills; it is not a matter of maintaining the status quo as if one were simply buying a franchise—which was in fact how many of the prospective buyers perceived the situation. In our opinion, the buyers were at most Single As, and the businesses required the skills of at least a Double A in order to be reinvented.

Often, the kind of buyer just profiled is the best available: they have money, some experience, and industry knowledge. However, our bet is that if the sale proceeded, they would go out of business within 24 months due to the mismatch between the entrepreneurial skills required by the situation and the skills they actually possessed. If this is so common, is there anything that can be done to change the odds of success?

Typically, nothing is done to address this disparity in skill levels because, frankly, it is not recognized. The company is sold, and when it declines, everyone suggests bringing back the original owner to save it. Rarely does this work, because the company's decline was usually due to the original owner in the first place. Even when this is not the case, the founding entrepreneur is often no longer interested in, or physically capable of, running the business again.

Instead, we think the situation calls for an economic development strategy designed to improve the buyers' entrepreneurial skills, such as individual business coaching. If timed properly (i.e., begun before the acquisition), and given sufficient resources to achieve its goal, such an intervention could close the gap, lead to an effective transition, and preserve the asset.

Timing is critical, which is why advanced planning is necessary. For example, one individual we know had a business that was worth $10 million when he died. He did not plan for his succession. Because he *was* the business, as is typical of a Single A entrepreneur, the family could only get $3 million for it when they tried to sell it. By the time a deal was reached, they only received $1 million, meaning that the business essentially lost $9 million in value, and a reasonably significant business asset was greatly diminished, representing a loss to the community.

Examples like this (which are all too common to practitioners in the field) indicate that there is much work that needs to be done with the owners to get them ready to exit their business and turn it over to someone else. This can be an emotionally charged event in their life. A proactive approach can be beneficial to everyone.

While this is a fairly complex situation with multiple aspects, it is increasingly the kind of scenario facing economic developers today. Let us explore how this economic development strategy should be designed to produce a positive return-on-investment. The following discussion is specific, but speculative.

Using very rough calculations, let us assume that it would cost $75,000 to operate a succession planning seminar and provide coaching for a period of six months to at least 30 entrepreneurs who are interested in selling their businesses. Let us also assume that it would cost $150,000 to provide in-depth coaching to 30 prospective entrepreneurs for a period of 18 to 24 months in order to develop their entrepreneurial skills (which have been assessed to be insufficient). Finally, let us assume administrative and legal costs of $75,000 over two years to facilitate the matches; we expect brokerage fees to be paid by the sellers. The total costs to operate this initiative over a two-year period would be $300,000.

On the benefit side, let us assume that only 50 percent of the 30 participants consummate deals for the sale of the business, and that of those 15 businesses, only 12 survive after the first year. Let us simplify by assuming that each business saves an average of five jobs and $5 million in revenue, all of which would have been lost had the businesses closed. That amounts to 60 jobs and $60 million saved, as well as the wealth produced from the sale of the businesses that is now available to be spent or invested in the community.

The return-on-investment of this economic development initiative could be measured in several ways. First, we could use annual sales revenue divided by the program cost: $60 million divided by $300,000 (spent over two years), or a return of 200 times the dollars spent. Or we could calculate the cost per job saved: $280,000 divided by 60 jobs, or a one-time expenditure of $5,000 per job.

Anyone is free to challenge the preceding assumptions or calculations. What is important is not getting the numbers exactly right (they are estimates and best guesses), but rather the discipline of specifying the requirements necessary to produce a successful outcome and a return-on-investment. If we proceed with this initiative, we now have a set of targets for participation and results for which a program manager can be held accountable. Instead of just trying something and seeing what happens, we have engineered a performance-oriented operation. By approaching the implementation as a well-designed experiment, we will learn about the accuracy of our assumptions and can improve our operations and our estimates over time.

SCENARIO 2: ADDRESSING WEAKNESS IN MANUFACTURER'S LOCAL SUPPLIER BASE

A regional manufacturer is quickly outgrowing the capacity and capability of its local base of suppliers. Their advisors are suggesting moving the work overseas to China, which would result in the loss of approximately 45 well-paying jobs and the closure of at least half of the 16 suppliers. The traditional thinking says that the decision is cut and dried—go with the lowest cost producer. The transaction will benefit the manufacturer in the end, and hopefully, the lower prices of offshore production combined with the growth in customer demand, and resulting business expansion, will somehow make up for the lost jobs. That is just the cost of doing business in an increasingly competitive world.

This is a very limited perspective—it uses zero-sum thinking and relies on hope rather than effort to produce net positive outcomes. Using the Pipeline as a lens through which to view the situation helps us see that the problem has to do with the skill limitations of the suppliers, who are largely technicians. Instead of accepting out-sourcing offshore as the only solution, we suggest the development of the supplier base through coaching to improve their entrepreneurial skills, combined with technical assistance in the form of specific initiatives like lean manufacturing and supervisory training and financing, if required.

If successful, this strategy has the potential to not only meet the manufacturer's need for increased capacity and capability, but to preserve the businesses and jobs in the region. It can also be achieved within a reasonable timeframe; anyone that has actually done outsourcing abroad knows that it takes significant lead time to set up such operations. More importantly, developing the skills of these firms increases their ability to go after new customers and grow their businesses. They are no longer captive to a single client. As these suppliers become economically stronger and technically more sophisticated, they will be of greater value to their original manufacturing customer.

What does it take for a community to get this done? In most supplier development programs in the United States operated by large companies, the coaching and technical assistance is provided by an executive on loan from the manufacturer or end customer. After all, the thinking goes, the client knows what they need and would seem to be in the best position to help because they have the most to gain.

In our experience, such programs rarely work; their flaws are due to faults built into their design, not necessarily their execution. First of all, the executives on loan are almost *never* entrepreneurs. As corporate managers they are used to having resources at their command and have rarely faced the conditions that their suppliers live with daily. Second, coaching to develop new skills requires a relationship of trust, and suppliers do not believe they will receive advice that is unbiased and in their best interest from a customer, whose interests in the best of circumstances are different, and in the worst, adversarial. Third, the assumption that the customer's knowledge base is relevant is questionable; just because they consume what the supplier produces doesn't mean they know how to make it in the first place. Finally, supplier development programs rarely focus on developing new skills. They are usually oriented to performance enhancements—changes that will facilitate the suppliers' ability to meet the contractual needs of the manufacturer—but not much beyond that.

Instead, we recommend an independent source of coaching as well as technical and financial assistance. The support should not be narrowly designed to meet the requirements of a particular contract but to increase their capability more broadly, enabling these suppliers to pursue other market opportunities as well.

This approach could be applied in other types of supplier situations. One of the problems with set-aside programs in this country is that they only provide half the support needed by women and minority firms, for example. Without also helping them to develop the skills necessary to operate the additional business, letting bigger contracts simply puts the firms out of business faster. In considering this option, a set of performance specifications and a cost-benefit analysis, similar to the one completed for the business succession scenario above, should be developed. This would enable someone to test the conditions under which such an initiative would be effective and produce a positive return-on-investment.

SCENARIO 3: PURSUING HIGH-IMPACT FIRMS

Under pressure for immediate results, many economic development initiatives focus on "high-impact clients."[3] This means utilizing performance enhancement strategies to work exclusively with high-growth (usually technology-oriented), later stage, "second-stage" or venture backable companies, referred to as gazelles, that are expected to generate very substantial results in terms of revenues and jobs in extremely short periods of time. This focus on high-impact clients reflects the tendency to seize on a single idea as the answer to a community's economic problems and pursue that idea at the expense of all others. While this approach has the benefit of being easy to understand, it also has a number of serious flaws.

This strategy assumes that economic developers are capable of effectively evaluating opportunities and picking winners, much as venture capitalists attempt to do. "Even after extensive due diligence and monitoring, many venture capital investments yield disappointing returns: One study of venture capital portfolios by Venture Economics, Inc. reported that about 7 percent of investments accounted for more than 60 percent of the profits, while fully one-third resulted in a partial or total loss."[4] A more commonly cited statistic is that no more than 1 in 100 venture capital investments yield a "home run"—that is, significant returns on investment. This is a very challenging strategy to implement, and the expectation of a high level of performance by the public or nonprofit sectors, who typically undertake it, is unrealistic. Reliance on gross generalizations such as which sectors are "hot" (e.g., wireless, biotechnology, telecommunications, etc.)—a typical substitute for good judgment—has also proven to be unsuccessful.

This approach is risky and prone to failure. This form of behavior, known as the "big opportunity" trap (or putting all of one's eggs in one basket), is commonly engaged in by large corporations as well as communities.[5] As Rita McGrath, an entrepreneurship researcher and educator, points out, "companies that make huge, irreversible investments as single attempts at innovation, risk suffering losses that are enormous compared to losses risked by companies that engage in many smaller initiatives. Consider Exxon's failed multibillion dollar venture into oil shale, as compared to the continuous innovations introduced by 3M."[6] It also increases risk by eliminating all other promising opportunities, the potential for small opportunities to grow into big ones (which is actually how big opportunities come into being), and the opportunity to learn from failure.

In its exclusive focus on high-tech firms and the elusive gazelle, this strategy has fallen prey to hype. According to David Birch, close to 30 percent of all gazelles are in the wholesale and retail trades; another

30 percent are in services. Of the gazelles on 2000's *Inc.* 500, only 47 percent were in computers or other electronics. "Most growth companies are in low-tech or traditional industries," concluded researcher Emil E. Malizia.[7]

An ideological focus on a single type of business to the exclusion of others is a form of gambling. It undermines the Pipeline by promoting a winner-take-all mentality and starving the other segments of the Pipeline of much needed investment. It assumes that financial success will trickle down to others in the community, although it is never explained how this will happen, nor is it clear that the necessary connections to ensure that this occurs are, in fact, ever made.

Using the Pipeline as a lens through which to look at this situation, several questions emerge. First, it is unclear to what segment of the Pipeline the term "high-impact clients" applies. Proponents of this strategy seem to be referring to Double A entrepreneurs whose firms are in the Expansion Stage of the business life cycle, although it may also apply to firms at the Mature Stage at the Double A skill level. For example, an approach called Economic Gardening is said to "focus on helping so-called second-stage companies with 10 to 50 employees and revenue of $1 million to $25 million—local businesses that have survived at least five years and are growing revenue and adding employees."[8] These criteria certainly fit with these Pipeline segments, but not all performance efforts are as clear.

A more significant and troubling question is why these firms need to be targets of public policy or investments of public resources. Firms occupying these two Pipeline segments are certainly able to pay for financial and technical assistance themselves. By working with them, nonprofit economic development organizations seem to be competing directly with the private sector and diverting scarce resources away from other entrepreneurs who need them and have fewer options for securing them.

It is also unclear what, and whose, needs economic developers are trying to address, what assistance is being provided, and why these firms can't obtain these resources on their own. There is no shortage of private-sector businesses capable of delivering the necessary financial and technical assistance, no matter where these high-impact firms are located in the United States.

This is not just an equity issue; it is also an efficiency issue. The question is: where in the Pipeline is it most cost-beneficial to work? This question must be answered first, before a target is chosen. Economic developers and public officials should be required to explain why resources should be going to support these firms instead of being used in other parts of the Pipeline. Otherwise, these firms might just be earning windfall profits.

One reason why this tactic is being pursued is that economic development agencies are engaged in the growing practice of "creaming" or "skimming." Rather than having to develop entrepreneurs and enterprises to the point where they yield high impacts, which takes time, these organizations can capture ventures that have already "made it" and ride their coattails to short-term economic development success. Thus, they are focused on high-impact clients, because it gives them good performance numbers to report to their funders and political supporters and to justify their existence. In this explanation, this strategy addresses the needs of the technical and financial assistance providers, not the clients.

We can however, imagine decisions to focus on high-impact clients that are based on sound, strategic reasons, grounded in the logic of the Pipeline. For example, let us suppose that the targeted firm is the manufacturer described in Scenario 2. In that case, assistance to such a firm could have a direct multiplier effect on its entire supply chain. The economic impact could be significant. Or let us suppose that the targeted business is located in a high-profile segment of the Pipeline occupied by few other businesses in the region. Its success could have a developmental multiplier effect on other entrepreneurs by serving as a role model and a reference as to what can possibly be achieved by more highly skilled entrepreneurs. Or the firm could be part of a market/industry cluster (to be discussed later in this chapter) and could, as a result, produce an economic as well as a developmental multiplier. Note, however, that these choices are strategic and systemic; they have both a positive cost-benefit ratio and a favorable impact on the rest of the Pipeline. They must be carefully planned in advance and executed with an eye to ensuring the proper connections are made.

There could be other reasons as well for the selection of these particular targets. Perhaps, while these firms are growing, their entrepreneurs are stuck at a skill level that is not sufficient, and they are entering a Crash Point. If the fact that such a promising business with an obviously strong market opportunity is faced with a problem like this, and it is known to others in the community (e.g., economic developers, bankers, equity investors, etc.), then it would be to everyone's advantage if economic developers could help.

Changes that require transformations are much more difficult for individual entrepreneurs to observe in themselves and navigate for and by themselves. As a result, they can then be much less willing to engage in and pay for this kind of support. In contrast, performance enhancements are more concrete, clearer in terms of the need and the benefit. Entrepreneurs are far more prepared to engage in these efforts and pay for them. They should be expected to do so.

Perhaps the changes entrepreneurs need to make are of the incubation or transformation variety. It could be in the community's interest to help motivate their high-impact entrepreneurs to engage in this work, in order to continue their development as entrepreneurs. Peer groups, such as the ones operated by the Lowe Foundation from Michigan, could be useful for this purpose.[9] Coaching by more experienced entrepreneurs would also be beneficial.

The problem with an economic development strategy that focuses on high-impact clients is that it is not sustainable. What happens when the community can find no more businesses to work with that fit the criteria? The major complaint of service providers with a high-impact focus is that there are not enough entrepreneurs with whom to work.[10] What should the community do for its next act?

This complaint about lacking entrepreneurs is simply not true. There are plenty of entrepreneurs, just not enough that fit the providers' highly exclusive definition. The solution to this predicament is to reach deeper into the Pipeline in order to develop entrepreneurs and create more high-impact firms.

SCENARIO 4: ENCOURAGING MATURE COMPANIES TO BE MORE ENTREPRENEURIAL

Most economic developers leave mature companies out of their strategic considerations, believing that there is little that they can or should do for these entrepreneurs and enterprises. We believe this to be a missed opportunity that should be aggressively pursued. Communities can encourage mature firms to become more entrepreneurial by supporting an economic development strategy aimed at encouraging intrapreneurship within companies. As they mature, too many companies lose the entrepreneurial edge by which they achieved their success. The solution is to distribute the entrepreneurial skills and behavior throughout the organization; in other words, applying the Pipeline to the individual corporation.

Many larger companies have a divisional structure or a set of individual lines of business. Many leaders we have met want these lines of business to be operated by individuals who think of themselves as entrepreneurs, not as employees. The CEOs want these individuals to assume profit and loss responsibility and to spend their time thinking as owners (of course, to properly be motivated, these individuals need to share in the returns from their efforts). Some executives have even expressed to us an interest in selling these lines to their employees as part of their succession plan. Others have explored the possibility of setting up certain employees as partners in their own business, pursuing a market opportunity that is of interest to the new entrepreneur and the firm. We have also suggested that corporations recruit successful retired entrepreneurs to pursue opportunities that they (the corporations) have already identified but have no one to run.

An added benefit to the spread of entrepreneurship throughout larger firms is the creation of new opportunities for entrepreneurs to learn and to develop new skills. The entire community and region would benefit from this. Mature companies rarely have the necessary infrastructure in place to support intrapreneurs. Economic developers could make available to them the same system of coaching and technical as well as financial assistance that they have put in place for local entrepreneurs and expand their clientele.

INTERLUDE: NOTICING A BIFURCATION IN THE PIPELINE

A Pipeline analysis we did in western Michigan revealed a bifurcation or division. When asked about the availability of financing for their ventures, entrepreneurs split evenly on the answer. We couldn't make sense of it, until we sorted them according to their positions in the Pipeline. That distribution revealed that entrepreneurs in the upper right-hand corner of the Pipeline (see Figure 8.1)—from the Double A skill level up and from the Expansion Stage in the life cycle on—which we refer to as the Zone of Maximization, consistently stated that there was more than enough financing in the region to fund their ventures. By contrast, all entrepreneurs in the lower left-hand corner of the Pipeline

FIGURE 8.1.
Bifurcation in the Pipeline

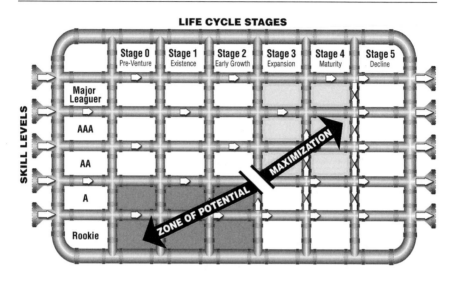

(from the Single A skill level down and from the Pre-Venture through Early Growth Stages), known as the Zone of Potential, stated that there is no money available in this region for their ventures. In other words, the answer depends on which part of the Pipeline you are in. This pattern is true for many types of technical assistance as well.

Analysis of the supply side confirmed that in this region, there is essentially one system for financing entrepreneurs in the Zone of Maximization (a specific set of firms offering financing and technical assistance), and another system for financing entrepreneurs in the Zone of Potential (i.e., family and friends, savings, credit cards, and sweat equity). The formal financial resources available to entrepreneurs in this latter segment were extremely limited. We saw no evidence of either entrepreneurs or service providers from these two zones crossing the chasm to the other region (although the time period over which we were able to draw our conclusions was limited).

This experience left us wondering how many community or regional Pipelines are bifurcated, without any bridge to connect the populations from these two different zones. The thinking from the previous examples leads us to believe that it may be more common than we would expect. This presents significant problems for those firms in the Zone of Potential and for communities that lack high-impact clients in which to invest.

SCENARIO 5: WORKING THE ZONE OF POTENTIAL

A large number of the firms in every community tend to get stuck in a couple of different segments in the Pipeline. Rookie entrepreneurs tend to get stuck at the Existence Stage in the business life cycle; Single A entrepreneurs tend to get stuck at the Early Growth Stage (the so-called mom and pop shops). Firms led by Rookie entrepreneurs tend to crash if they try to move to the Early Growth Stage without first increasing their skills. Firms led by Single A entrepreneurs tend to crash if they try to move to the Expansion Stage, without first increasing their skill level. The problem for an entrepreneur that reaches this particular Pipeline segment is that no provider from the Zone of Maximization will reach back to work with them; and no provider from the Zone of Potential is capable of working with them. This is a no-man's land for Single As, and, as economic development practitioners, we haven't done enough to figure out how to help them (see Figure 8.2).

FIGURE 8.2.
Dynamics in the Zone of Potential

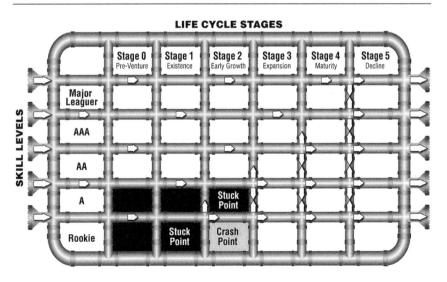

These patterns lead us to two questions, because these Stuck Points and Crash Points seem to be so common:

- What is the cost of these dysfunctions in the Pipeline, in economic and human terms?
- What would the value be of an economic development strategy designed to help entrepreneurs move out of the Stuck Points and avoid the Crash Points?

It is economically and socially inefficient to allow such unnecessary failures in these segments of the Pipeline. Many wasted resources and lost opportunities could be avoided by strategic initiatives in the Pipeline that would address these problems in a systemic and proactive manner.

For example, we had been urging one entrepreneur with whom we worked to hire a chief financial officer (CFO) for his firm, in order to establish greater control over his costs and to empower his employees to make better decisions based on the information this position could make available. This was a Single A entrepreneur whose business was in the Early Growth Stage. For various reasons, he did not do so for five years. When he did hire the CFO, he saw a significant increase in his profitability in the first year, even with a decline in total revenues, an increase that more than paid for the cost of the new CFO in the first five months. We conservatively estimate that the five-year delay in hiring cost him a total of more than $1 million dollars in lost profit, representing a significant loss in wealth. By adding to his management team, this entrepreneur's skill was significantly enhanced.

Some policymakers and economic developers assume that the businesses in the Zone of Potential are not economically significant and are therefore not important. That may be true of an individual firm, but not when these assets are considered collectively. These entrepreneurs and enterprises also provide valuable services, without which much of the work in our communities would not get done.

As a result, there is a large number of opportunities for small but individually significant gains in this zone of the Pipeline, gains that when aggregated can be huge. If 300 firms each hired one employee, the employment impact would be tremendous. If each of those firms became more profitable, paid higher wages as well as benefits, increased their tax payments, and began to take home more disposable income for their families, the economy would be transformed. And as entrepreneurs and their enterprises made the transition from the Zone of Potential to the Zone of Maximization, the community would be making more "cream."

We believe the benefits of investing in entrepreneurs in the Pipeline's Zone of Potential to be high. If the initiatives are well-designed, implemented, and connected to the Zone of Maximization, the benefits will far exceed the costs. This approach succeeds in linking entrepreneurship and community economic development in a productive way.

SCENARIO 6: WHAT TO DO WITH ARTISTS, CRAFTSPEOPLE, DESIGNERS, AND ENGINEERS?

Artists, craftspeople, designers, and engineers are all members of the creative economy. In some regions, they can make up a significant percentage of the employment base. As our economy becomes increasingly knowledge-driven, the importance of these occupations to innovation is growing. The question is: how can regions utilize these people as engines of economic development?

The traditional answer is: turn them into entrepreneurs so that they can start their own businesses. This is clearly one possibility, but in many cases it is an option with a low probability of success, as the following example suggests. An engineer starts his own company because he loves a certain kind of technical work. He does it better than everyone else, so why shouldn't he reap the rewards of his efforts, rather than be satisfied with a job? While he is not excited about the business management tasks and responsibilities, he nonetheless learns and performs them. As his business grows and becomes successful, he finds that he is spending precious little of his time on the work that motivated him to start the business in the first place. He grows increasingly frustrated and unhappy. Seeing no way out of this dilemma, he closes the business and returns to work for someone else.

We have seen this scene replayed countless times by individuals in all of these professions. Assisting them to develop entrepreneurial skills would not help. In some cases, they are not capable of performing them well. In others, that's not the issue—it is just not something they desire to do. Their passion lies elsewhere.

Is there a solution to this dilemma or are only a few in the creative economy destined to be successful as entrepreneurs? Viewed through the Pipeline, our suggestion is that this engineer develop his entrepreneurial skills by creating a team, of which he becomes a member, not the leader. Our recommendation is that he becomes the chief technology officer (CTO), reporting to a chief executive officer, whom, as the owner of the company, he hires.

This is a complex suggestion, but it can work—with the proper preparation and understanding. The engineer has two roles to perform: one as owner of the company and the second as an employee with a particular set of responsibilities. Of course there is plenty of room for conflict between these two roles, but because each of us is required to perform multiple roles every day as husbands and wives, parents, employees, and citizens, and do so successfully, we have plenty of experience to draw upon.

The engineer is motivated to take on the role of chief technology officer, because his passion lies in that role. But as owner of the business, he can continue to control and benefit from the financial asset that he has created. As owner, he chooses the individual he wants to lead his business and sets the parameters of that role. As CTO, he is obligated to perform his role under the direction and the control of the individual he placed in the position of CEO. He now becomes a member of the CEO's management team. If the owner is smart and has chosen well, the CEO will be someone he will respect and whose decisions about the business he will be willing to follow.

Choosing a leader and making the transition to these new roles requires a great deal of attention, deliberation, and humility. We have all observed the owner who has run through multiple CEOs. This situation may be due to the fact that the owner is someone with whom it is impossible to get along; or it could be that he is someone that didn't do the work necessary to make a good decision. If the latter is the case, the situation can be corrected.

The proper timing of the transition is critical to its success. Few companies, unless well-financed, can afford to hire a CEO in advance of the cash flow necessary to support it. But it rarely takes a genius to proactively determine the point at which a company will need such expertise. If sales are growing at a particular rate, then the time when the shift needs to occur can be predicted. If the owner does his homework, recruits a CEO after due deliberation, and mentally prepares himself, then he can easily pull the switch to have the CEO start when the right moment arrives.

When, however, owners wait until the time they can afford to hire a CEO to start the recruiting process, they usually find themselves in an acute state of crisis, which presents much more serious impediments to navigating a successful transition. An understanding of the Pipeline, and particularly the stages in the business life cycle, helps one see the sequence and timing of the needs as the business develops, and enables one to anticipate such situations.

The players also need to be prepared to manage the conflict that is a natural part of any relationship, but that will be particularly challenging with these roles. For example, what if the owner/engineer is someone who likes new technical challenges and is always willing to take on new clients on the basis of how interesting their problems are to him? But the CEO, knowing that the best customers are the ones who pay well and pay on time, insists on rejecting a particular prospect because they don't meet those criteria. Who will prevail? If the roles and relationships are right, it should be the CEO in most cases. His choices will increase the value of the business. Coaching can be particularly helpful. Properly managed, we have seen this arrangement work quite successfully. Economic developers could create a coaching program for this purpose or facilitate matches to existing coaching practices.

This scenario also contains the seeds of an idea for what to do with the numerous small artists, crafts producers, or designers that inhabit the Pipeline segment of Rookie entrepreneurs at the Existence Stage. We recommend that 12 to 15 of them be placed in an incubator whose purpose is to provide them with the business and operational tasks that they lack in the form of a manager and assistant whose time would be distributed equally among them. This manager would be responsible for marketing, bookkeeping, packaging and shipping, and so on. We are not talking about the arms-length transactions that exist between the craft producer or artisan, for example, and a particular distribution channel—a Web catalog or retail outlet. Instead, we are referring to a closer business partnership. The key to success would be the strength of that relationship and the willingness and ability of the artist/designer to accept those terms. The clients would have to have the personal maturity to function well on a team.

Those individuals who are willing and able to use this as a stepping stone to grow themselves and their business would graduate from the incubator to either operate on their own or to participate in a newly constructed incubator initiative for Single A craftspeople at the Early Growth Stage. Those that stay would be expected to operate a more profitable and successful business in their segment of the Pipeline, which is a positive outcome.

SCENARIO 7: MARKET OR INDUSTRY CLUSTERS

Over the last 10 years, cluster analysis has become a popular approach to identifying concentrations of various industries within a geographic area, which can then become targets of cost-effective economic development strategies. Its appeal is a function of its holism, its focus on a regional level, and its potential for impact, as well as economies of scale.

However, despite its popularity, clusters have failed to live up to this potential. We believe this is because it is a data analysis tool that provides very limited insight for action. There are two problems with cluster analysis. First, it assumes that entrepreneurs and enterprises within a cluster have similar needs, that in terms of services, one size will fit all. This is clearly false. While the label used to describe a particular need, such as "training," for example, will be the same across the entire population, what that label represents in terms of actual content will be completely different across the population.

The Pipeline provides an effective way of understanding this point, as we have been explaining throughout this book. Business plans, for instance, will differ in every segment of the Pipeline—in the way they are generated, in their structure, and in terms of the need(s) they are addressing. The same thing is true for financing, as well as every other need entrepreneurs and businesses have.

This undermines the much-hoped-for economies of scale and scope. Cluster analysis by itself is unable to reveal any single policy or programmatic "lever" that will produce benefits across the entire cluster in a cost-effective way. Something more is needed. We think cluster analysis must be combined with an analysis of the cluster's Pipeline in order to identify opportunities for both growth and development.

The second problem is that cluster analysis is looking for future opportunities by searching data that represent the past. This will tell us about established clusters, but it offers no way to identify emerging or potential clusters. Because big opportunities were all once small opportunities, it would be of great benefit if we could identify the emergence of new clusters and provide assistance in order to increase their probabilities of success. The identification of emerging clusters cannot be done on a macro basis by an analysis of aggregate data. They can only be found by dropping down into the forest and examining the individual trees. A Pipeline analysis offers a means of achieving that microlevel focus, while at the same time linking the results up to the whole.

By facilitating a microlevel focus, an analysis of a cluster's Pipeline would also give us enough real data to identify opportunities to seed potential clusters and interfirm networks, from the bottom up. Powerful insights come from highly structured knowledge about the daily challenges of entrepreneurs and their businesses. Economic development practitioners can use this information to test the demand for new initiatives.

Finally, a Pipeline approach would give cluster-oriented practitioners a dimension they are missing entirely—a focus on the development of entrepreneurs and their skills. The typical cluster strategy targets only one dimension of the Pipeline—the enterprise. As we noted earlier in this book, this assumes that the company moves through the stages of the business life cycle smoothly and on its own. Because this is not the case, cluster strategies are vulnerable to all of the Stuck Points, Crash Points, disconnects, and other dysfunctions that occur when little or no attention is paid to developing the skills of entrepreneurs and entrepreneurial teams. Combining cluster analysis with a Pipeline analysis has the power to produce more strategic and effective implementations within a cluster.

SCENARIO 8: GAPS IN TECHNICAL AND FINANCIAL ASSISTANCE

In many communities, there are gaps in the availability of technical and financial assistance, as these two examples illustrate:

- Entrepreneurs who have successfully graduated from microenterprise programs have reported being satisfied with their experience, but they are left afterwards with a sense of being in limbo, not having anywhere to go for support in taking their business to the next level. For example, entrepreneurs from a midsized southern city had been participating in a microenterprise program for up to 11 years and were still Rookies running Existence Stage businesses. They loved the warmth and caring of the program, but they couldn't grow because they couldn't attract bank financing.
- One particular northeastern U.S. city has often been described as good at starting firms but not at growing them to maturity. At the same time, local venture capitalists and others have complained about the lack of "good" entrepreneurs in which to invest.[11]

An analysis of aggregated secondary statistics on startups would not reveal either of these problems; nor would it be capable of suggesting potential solutions. However, they can be diagnosed using the Pipeline. Our explanation for these patterns is that they represent gaps in technical and financial assistance that are specific to particular segments in the Pipeline in these communities. Entrepreneurs who progress to these segments then get stuck there for lack of assistance to move their businesses forward. These gaps in assistance contribute to breaks in or fragmentation of the Pipeline, which then disrupts the flow and volume.

In the example of microenterprise programs, graduation, interpreted as a measure of success by service providers and funders, can in many cases simply be another level where entrepreneurs stall in their development as they outgrow the assistance that has been provided by that particular organization. In terms of our diagram, we interpret this as a move by an entrepreneur from somewhere below the Pipeline in terms of skill level (which we refer to as the Sub-Pipeline) and the Pre-Venture Stage in the business life cycle (probably an informal, home-based, or underground business) to the Rookie skill level and Existence Stage of the business (and still an informal business). These entrepreneurs are now looking for help in moving to the Single A skill level and the Early Growth Stage in the life cycle (see Figure 8.3).

Some foundations, in keeping with their philanthropic missions, tend to exacerbate this fragmentation in the Pipeline by their exclusive emphasis on "low-income communities." They want people to work their way out of this stratum and be able to join the economic mainstream. To do so, members of the community need a ladder from where they presently are to where they want to be. Yet, many such programs limit their attention to members of this segment of the economy. With the best of intentions, this merely creates a path to nowhere or another "Stuck Point." Without any linkage to the broader economy, low-income entrepreneurs will continue to be isolated and endure limited success.

The situation in the northeastern city could be explained by this hypothesis: There are many Single A entrepreneurs who start firms, and plenty of financing available for Triple A entrepreneurs, but the support structure for Double A entrepreneurs and the bridges between Single A and Double A as well as between Double A and Triple A are weak or nonexistent.

In point of fact, discussions with entrepreneurs confirm the impression that there is a disruption in the ladder of development and the infrastructure of support in that city. Many Double A entrepreneurs must seek financing outside the region, because local investors are

FIGURE 8.3.
Breaks in the Skill Ladder

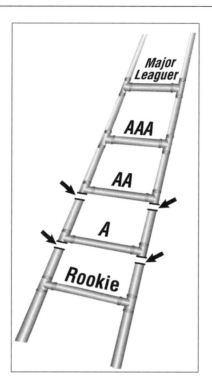

unwilling to invest in them until they are at the Triple A level. In exchange, the entrepreneurs are asked to move to the out-of-town investors' location, so that they can be closely observed and supported.[12] If that is true (and such statements and conclusions can be substantiated by further research), the diagnosis suggests a clear and targeted local enterprise development strategy. In other words, using the Pipeline framework, the issue can be translated into a question capable of being researched and on which action can be taken.

Regions and states have responded to these perceived gaps by establishing special initiatives. But without having properly analyzed the nature of these gaps, they are making serious mistakes. For example, in the early years of this decade, many states seized upon venture capital (VC) as the economic development strategy of choice, thinking that the lack of VC financing was the obstacle to successful growth companies (largely high-tech). Like many places, one state with which we are familiar distributed money to a number of venture capital funds in order to encourage them to locate in the state and make investments. After seven years, few investments were made; in fact, one fund returned the entire amount to the state, unspent. What went wrong?

In terms of the Pipeline, venture capitalists commonly invest in Triple A entrepreneurs; they look for individuals or teams that have already demonstrated the necessary skills—they do not want to spend the time or the money to invest in anyone's development.[13] This state had a paucity of entrepreneurs at the Triple A level; in fact, they had a very limited number of Double As. Many of the Triple As that the state had produced left for other regions of the country, just as in the case of the northeastern city described above, because the necessary technical and financial assistance did not exist at home. So there was a mismatch between the market and the financial instrument.

The clients or deal flow that the venture capitalists expected did not materialize, because it did not exist. On the other hand, the kind of financing needed by the entrepreneurs and firms that did exist was not there either. Both Single A and Double A entrepreneurs that constituted the bulk of the Pipeline population in this state were still struggling to find sources of financing. There was a mismatch between venture capitalists' expectations and the needs of the local entrepreneurs.

Given conditions of the state's Pipeline, this was the wrong economic development strategy. One could say that it was the right strategy for the wrong part of the Pipeline—that segment had no members in it. Or it was the right strategy at the wrong time in the development of that state's Pipeline—in other words, the strategy was employed in the wrong sequence. If the state were committed, for some reason, to starting a venture capital fund, it should first have made investments in order to develop a Pipeline of potential customers for that approach. In our view, they should first have invested in working with the existing Double A entrepreneurs in order to move a sufficient number of them to the Triple A level, thus making them qualified for venture capital financing. Had the state conducted a Pipeline analysis, it would have been able to realize this problem, in advance of committing the funds. Those same funds could have been put to more productive uses in other Pipeline segments, with lost opportunities avoided.

For this reason, gross analyses or broad judgments, such as the conclusion that a state or region needs venture capital funding because its firms lack external sources of financing, are seriously flawed. Without a deeper understanding of various methods of financing, and a grounded understanding of the Pipeline of the area of focus, one cannot possibly determine what strategy to apply, when and where, let alone expect positive results.

In another area of the country where we were involved, there was an attempt to diagnose the reason why farmers were unable to obtain the capital they needed to expand their businesses. Some were arguing that the problem was a lack of capital and were proposing to establish a fund. After speaking to the banks in the area, we concluded that the supply of debt capital was more than sufficient; the problem was on the demand side. Farmers, we found, were unwilling or unable (or both) to prepare the financial statements, particularly a balance sheet, necessary to obtain financing.[14] This was the heart of the issue, and any discerning economic developer would first want to determine why before implementing a solution. Clearly, another loan fund would not have been the answer.

As we have argued before, diagnosis must precede the choice of an economic development strategy. The analysis of a region's Pipeline should also explore the existence of any gaps in technical and financial assistance. It is not good enough to establish that there are Pipeline segments that are missing service providers. It must be demonstrated that there are unserved clients in those segments who are in need of the services being proposed, without which they will remain stuck. In other words, a gap analysis must establish market demand that, if addressed, will restore the flow and volume in the Pipeline.[15]

SCENARIO 9: ECONOMIC ADJACENCIES AS GROWTH OPPORTUNITIES

Increasingly, business strategists emphasize that companies must focus their energy and resources on their "core"—what they do well.[16] Any move to expand from the core should focus on business opportunities that are close to the core. These moves are called "adjacencies." For a business, selling existing products to a new customer segment, say in another region or another country, would constitute an adjacency move. Developing a new product that requires new equipment and personnel for a market one knows nothing about would not.

Research indicates that the further the new opportunity is from what you know and are good at, the higher the risk of failure. Because every adjacency strategy is a journey into the unknown, each step should be incremental and represent a manageable progression. That is the best way to increase the probabilities of success.

These same principles apply to the selection of opportunities to be pursued by a particular community or region. For example, the selective recruitment strategies presented in the previous chapter are based on attracting firms with capabilities that complement those already present in the Pipeline. If a community or region is to increase their probability of success, then they need to be clear about how far a particular opportunity is from the core of the businesses and service providers in their area, as well as from what they, themselves, know.

As an example, many policymakers and economic developers attempt to push communities to move from no-tech to high-tech without any intervening steps. This is both unrealistic and highly susceptible to failure. This is not to say that communities cannot move into high-tech. We are just arguing that such a target must be pursued in a sequential and realistic manner in order to increase the probability of success.

Economic developers must understand their community's Pipeline to determine what market opportunities would fit and what adjacencies to pursue. This point became clear to us when attempting to promote tech transfer opportunities in nanotechnology in a rural region with few technology firms. The project opened our eyes to the fact that the region clearly was not fertile ground for these efforts, *at that time,* and our efforts needed to focus on the kinds of opportunities that would help them get there *over* time. We needed to go back to the drawing board to figure out the sequence or progression of steps required to make the Pipeline more technologically oriented. For example, a good first step would be to introduce existing retail, manufacturing, and wholesale businesses to more high-tech tools to improve the productivity of their operations. This will create a user base that can then form the foundation for other high-tech forays, such as the development of proprietary software targeted to the needs of particular market niches.

There is a tie here to industry cluster strategies discussed earlier in this chapter. Enhancing an existing cluster ensures adjacency. When developing a new industry cluster, however, it is important to make certain that this cluster is complementary to existing business activity and does not require too great a stretch beyond local resource capacity. Combining cluster strategy with Pipeline strategy helps to guarantee adjacency in this latter scenario.

SCENARIO 10: RETAINING BUSINESSES IN THE REGION

There is an assumption that every business success is a win for the region. That is not true, as these two stories suggest. A venture capital forum in a southern city had a big success with one of its investments, and then the firm moved to Boston to get the additional capital it needed. Lycos, an early search engine company that was spun out of Carnegie Mellon University in Pittsburgh, Pennsylvania, is upheld as a major technology transfer and economic development success, but it too moved to Boston. These events demonstrate that companies will leave town in order to get the support they need to grow.

Although these firms were clearly success stories for their investors, when viewed from the Pipeline, they are seen as failures for their regions. Significant effort and resources were poured into companies that the region could not sustain. So these communities, in effect, served as farm systems for other Pipelines—in this case, the Boston region's Pipeline.

While there is no way to prevent this from happening, the more frequently it occurs, the more likely it indicates that opportunities are not being pursued in a systemic or strategic way. Rather than support any and all businesses with superstar potential, the Pipeline approach suggests that the community as a whole should focus on those businesses that fit with existing local businesses and available resources. That is, the businesses in which investments are made should complement local companies and local resource capacity. Firms that are socially as well as economically integrated into the area are less likely to leave.

SCENARIO 11: WHAT TO DO WITH THE
POPULATION BELOW THE PIPELINE?

How do we help members of the population that exist below the Pipeline—the poor, youth, and economically or socially disadvantaged groups, such as prisoners or ex-convicts? How do we prepare them to move into the Pipeline?[17] The issue here isn't about gender, skin color, age, ethnicity, or location. It is about overcoming the obstacles that cause these individuals to be disconnected from the economy.

The traditional response is to take low-income individuals and try to turn them into entrepreneurs. This has been advocated and applied to welfare-to-work programs, as an example. When viewed from the perspective of the Pipeline, this is an approach with a low probability for success. The reason, we believe, is that the distance between their current reality and the goal is too large.

One option to increase the success rate of such programs is to try harder: make the program more intensive, longer, provide more help and resources, make the requirements more demanding, and expend more effort keeping the clients in the system. Given the current economic climate, this is not necessarily an affordable option, nor do we believe that it is reflective of what this group needs. Another approach is to try to recruit better clients, but this option runs into the reality that the pool is extremely limited. Solely raising the criteria defeats the purpose of working at this level. We need to create a larger pool of better clients.

The solution is to work differently and smarter. Ultimately, we want to create more rungs on the ladder and create a reasonable track out of poverty. Using similar thinking to that described in chapter 6, where we examined how to work with Rookie entrepreneurs who have Triple A or Major League business aspirations, we suggest that the journey be broken up into discrete, manageable segments. We need to extend the Pipeline approach further and deeper.

We need to make even finer distinctions regarding the skills of individuals in the Sub-Pipeline (at levels below a Rookie).[18] There will be a small number of individuals that can make the transition to entrepreneurship directly (in other words, they could move from being on welfare to becoming a Rookie entrepreneur). If limited resources are to be expended efficiently, programs need to be very selective in order to produce a sufficiently high return-on-investment.[19] We could use succession opportunities at the lower end in the Pipeline (under the terms described in the first scenario in this chapter) to offer graduates business possibilities.

However, for individuals who do not fit this criterion (which will be most of them), other options must be developed that are more appropriate for their needs. While there is not sufficient space to discuss these options fully, it is important to note that these options should include a variety of elements that already exist, and some new initiatives that need to be packaged together to operate seamlessly. It will require elements from the educational system, the work-force development system, and health and social services.

Before these individuals can even consider entrepreneurship, they first need to establish some very basic life and financial management skills. They need to learn how to manage their living spaces, bank accounts, and livelihoods. Tools like Individual Development Accounts that encourage new behaviors, such as savings, will be helpful. These individuals need to become financially literate and repair their credit. This stage before a foray into entrepreneurship should consist of a series of learning opportunities and apprenticeships with entrepreneurs in various areas of interest. This would give individuals a chance to observe and build basic experiences before even trying to become a Rookie.

We believe that this sequence of development levels in the Sub-Pipeline should be applied to youth entrepreneurship as well. There are a few rare adolescents who will be capable of starting a real business; but we should not build an entire system around extraordinary people; otherwise it will fail to work effectively for the rest. In general, our youths are not yet ready to be part of the Pipeline. They are our wellspring or raw supply of new entrepreneurs. We must prepare them to participate in entrepreneurship, and that means finding ways to keep them in our communities. Developmental activities and learning opportunities or apprenticeships could be effective approaches to building bridges between their current reality and the Pipeline.

We need to experiment further with new approaches to the Sub-Pipeline, particularly in international settings, where huge parts of the population can be found at this level. These are often the so-called underground entrepreneurs. Some of this group is currently engaged in illegal economic transactions. It must be demonstrated to them that it can be much more fulfilling and profitable as well to apply their entrepreneurial motivation and latent talent to legitimate business activities. Others are merely trying to avoid government oversight and taxes. In our experience, this latter group can be convinced that obtaining licenses and paying taxes is a price well worth paying when one operates a thriving business. Once these underground entrepreneurs are brought into the light of day, the process of individual skill development and business growth can begin.

CONCLUSION

These scenarios have demonstrated how the Pipeline can be used to diagnose economic conditions within a community or region that are impeding the flow and volume of entrepreneurs and enterprises. This framework also helps us to design better strategic interventions to address these problems. By first reverse-engineering these options, we can evaluate their ability to hit their goals and achieve a positive return-on-investment before we make that investment. Performance measurement is not an afterthought in this approach; it is built into the very way of operating.

The Steps in a Pipeline Analysis

1. Collect data on the region's entrepreneurs and enterprises and sort these into the appropriate segments of the Pipeline.[20]
2. Compare the region's Pipeline to areas with similar as well as dissimilar but desirable characteristics, on a variety of dimensions. Where possible, examine changes over time.
3. Analyze strengths and weaknesses of, opportunities for, and threats to the region's Pipeline.
4. Develop a set of strategic options for improving the performance of the Pipeline in terms of volume and flow.
5. Evaluate the options.
6. Choose the best options and implement.
7. Monitor performance and engage in continuous improvement.

Principles of Pipeline Management

It should be remembered that nothing is more difficult than to establish a new order of things.

—Machiavelli, *The Prince*

The Pipeline of Entrepreneurs and Enterprises provides a framework for managing a community's business assets. It enables economic developers to be systemic, systematic, and strategic in their efforts to build community wealth and transform the local or regional economy. Economic developers can manage their business assets by managing the Pipeline. This chapter discusses the basic operating principles for Pipeline management.

SUMMARY LIST OF PRINCIPLES

1. Invest in developing entrepreneurs.
2. Build a community of entrepreneurs.
3. Have entrepreneurs lead the way.
4. Manage the Pipeline of Entrepreneurs and Enterprises as a portfolio of related assets.
5. Operate in a client-centered manner.
6. Invest in the conditions necessary to effectively manage the Pipeline of Entrepreneurs and Enterprises.
7. Reconceptualize the role of economic developers as change agents.

1. Invest in Developing Entrepreneurs

There are two views about what it means to invest in entrepreneurship. One believes in investing in the business or opportunity; the other believes in investing in the entrepreneur. As we explore the natural tension between these two perspectives, we will show that both approaches are necessary, but they must be connected and in balance.

Betting on Businesses

The perspective that calls for investment in the business is best exemplified by Scott Shane, an entrepreneurship researcher and educator, who in the conclusion to his recent book, *The Illusions of Entrepreneurship*, raises (and answers) the following question about the choice between two investment possibilities:

> In fact, you already know how to select the companies to bet on. Take, for example, the following two businesses:
>
> - A personal cleaning business started by an unemployed high school dropout that is pursuing the customers of another personal cleaning business, is capitalized with $10,000 of the founder's savings, and is set up as a sole proprietorship.
> - An Internet company that is started by a former Microsoft employee with fifteen years of experience in the software industry, an MBA and a master's degree in computer science, that is pursuing the next generation of Internet search, is capitalized with $250,000 in money from the founder and the Band of Angels in San Francisco, and is set up as a corporation.
>
> Which one would you put your resources behind? It's obvious that the second business has a far better chance of success than the first one and that, on average, we would be better off putting our resources into such businesses. Why, then are we encouraging and subsidizing the creation of businesses like the first one?[1]

In contrast to Shane, we do not believe that the choice is so clear. But before critiquing this perspective and answering his final question, let us make a few observations.

First, for Shane, although he describes the entrepreneur's background in each case, the investment decision is about the business, not the entrepreneurs. This can be confirmed by a careful reading of his language. Second, these choices are from two entirely different segments of the Pipeline; specifically, they represent entrepreneurs from two different skill levels—a Rookie and Double A, respectively. Even assuming that each business is at the same stage in the life cycle, we are clearly being asked to compare apples and oranges. Third, as a result, the terms of the choice or "bet" are quite unclear. We are supposedly being asked to determine which one will produce a better return-on-investment (ROI), but to what goal (what is the endpoint), in what time frame or payback period, and in what relative terms? If we invest $15,000 in the first business for a payback of $45,000 in three years, can we say that this ROI is somehow worse than making an investment of $100,000 in the second company and receiving $300,000 in three years?[2]

Fourth, when Shane asks "which one would *you* put your resources behind," the "you" whom he is addressing is unclear. He seems to be talking to at least two very different audiences. One is the individual investor looking for a financial return. Then, with the addition of his question about encouraging and subsidizing businesses like the first one, he seems to be directing his inquiry to a social investor—the public or its elected representatives. The difference is important; it determines whose pocket the money will come from.

As we noted in our discussion of high-impact clients in the previous chapter, it is unclear why the public or nonprofit sector should be called upon to support businesses of the second type. There are well-developed private sector markets for businesses in this segment of the Pipeline. On the surface, it is hard to see how additional support is justified.

One could also argue that if the first business is a good deal with a reasonable probability of success, then it too will be able to draw private sector investment. However, using our Pipeline analysis, we observe that the risk factors are higher given that this business is led by a Rookie.[3] As we have discussed in chapter 6, Rookies tend to get stuck in the Existence Stage, and, if their business grows beyond that, it will in all likelihood crash because the entrepreneur's skill level is not sufficient to avoid that outcome. So the additional risk in this segment of the Pipeline is caused by inadequate skills on the part of the entrepreneur—a dimension that is glossed over in Shane's analysis.

By contrast, the second business is most probably led by a Double A entrepreneur whose skills are sufficient for the task of growing the business to the Expansion or Maturity Stage, at which point, he could sell the business to a larger corporation or turn the management over to more highly skilled individuals. Both are successful outcomes for him and his investors.

Private sector funders are not prepared to underwrite the risk due to insufficient skill levels, nor are they typically willing to invest in developing those skills.[4] Venture capitalists have a well-known reputation for investing in businesses and quickly replacing the entrepreneur if he or she is incapable of performing at the required level.

We are not arguing that this is the wrong decision or that venture capitalists are not acting rationally and responsibly from their perspective. What we are saying is that from society's perspective, there is a rationale for making investments in the first situation Shane describes—investments in developing the skills of the entrepreneur, so that from the perspective of the Pipeline, we can increase the volume and flow of high-quality entrepreneurs, that is, making more cream (see chapter 7, page 113).

Shane presents us with a misleading choice, but it is extremely representative of how these decisions are commonly framed. The choice lacks the dimensions of skill level and time flow. It ignores any sense of dynamics, instead suggesting that the choice is a static one between a "good" entrepreneur (in our terms, more highly skilled) and a "bad" entrepreneur (one with few skills). He seems to suggest that there is no way for a bad entrepreneur to become a good entrepreneur. For him, that is not an option.

But Shane's comparison also does not explain where the good entrepreneur came from. He was not born with an MBA and 15 years of experience from Microsoft. The reality is that every entrepreneur starts off as a Rookie. This is an inviolable law of nature, like gravity. The story of the second business's entrepreneur is much richer; it has a history and depth. This entrepreneur probably started his entrepreneurial career as did so many of the male entrepreneurs we have met, by mowing grass, testing computer games, or something of this nature. In terms of their skills, everyone starts at the same point; the difference is what they do going forward.

Separating Out Types of Entrepreneurs

This division of entrepreneurs into different populations is extremely common. In an interesting commentary in the *Wall Street Journal*, Amar Bhide, another leading entrepreneurship researcher and educator, distinguishes between what he calls *ameliorative* entrepreneurship, championed by Mohammad Yunus, the 2007 Nobel Peace Prize winner and leading microenterprise advocate, and *transformative* entrepreneurship, advocated by Edmund Phelps, the 2007 Nobel Laureate in Economics. Transformative entrepreneurship refers to businesses that produce major changes in the economy in terms of productivity or market impact.

Bhide asks, "Economic development does wonders for peace, but what does micro-financed entrepreneurship really do for economic development? Can turning more beggars into basket weavers make Bangladesh less of a, well, basket case? A few small port cities or petro states aside, there is no historical precedent for sustained improvements in living standards without broad-base modernization and widespread improvements in productivity brought about by the dynamic entrepreneurship that Mr. Phelps celebrates."[5]

We believe this simple dichotomy hides a much more complex reality, which can be revealed when viewed through the Pipeline. It assumes that these two populations are isolated and distinct—in other words, that there can be no movement by entrepreneurs from one segment of the Pipeline to another.

Is it not possible for some percentage of those engaged in ameliorative entrepreneurship to utilize these opportunities as stepping stones to engage in transformative opportunities? We are not arguing that this could happen all at once, but it could be one result of an entrepreneurial career or journey. We believe any argument against the possibility of such movement defies evidence to the contrary, defies logic, and is arrogantly blind to the limitations of our own knowledge. Who are any of us to claim to be able to judge someone's potential, simply on the basis of the opportunities they are currently pursuing?

For that matter, are these arguments, in any of their various incarnations, suggesting that we are incapable of doing anything to facilitate the journey from ameliorative to transformative entrepreneurship—to increase the flow from one skill level to another? We think that the more relevant question is: what does it take to do this and do we have the resources and willpower to make it happen?

If indeed we are right that all entrepreneurs begin as Rookies, then one will see even transformative entrepreneurs "recapitulate" the process of ameliorative entrepreneurs. When we review what we've heard entrepreneurs say about their first entrepreneurial experiences, we find that they were all engaged in activities that in and of themselves would certainly not constitute anything transformative. This was just an early stage in their development; if considered the sum total of all they had the potential to accomplish, the world would be a much poorer place.

The Pipeline helps put discussions about these various populations of entrepreneurs in perspective and to show how they are related. It helps us redefine stereotypical labels that preclude development into functional categories that facilitate it instead. It suggests that, as in any system, all parts of the Pipeline are important to the unique character of the whole.

Investing in Opportunities versus Investing in Entrepreneurs

This discussion helps illustrate two different ways of investing in entrepreneurship: investing to capture an opportunity and investing to develop an entrepreneur. Let us explore the first option and then the second, in more detail.

The opportunity-focused approach does not ignore entrepreneurs or their skill levels; it simply concentrates on finding the right people, not on developing them. As "Arthur Rock, a venture capital legend associated with the formation of such companies as Apple, Intel, and Teledyne, states, 'I invest in people, not ideas.' Rock also has said, 'If you can *find good people* [emphasis added], if they're wrong about the product, they'll make a switch, so what good is it to understand the product that they're talking about in the first place?'"[6] In our language, good entrepreneurs are ones whose skill levels match what is required to capture the market opportunity.

This emphasis on the opportunity can be observed particularly in the fields of technology transfer and technology commercialization. In addition, venture capitalists and community venture funds are increasingly seeking successful entrepreneurs who are available (free agents, currently without a business) to pursue promising market opportunities that either they have identified or that less skilled entrepreneurs have brought to them. The challenge here is to match the right entrepreneur with the right opportunity. And while the challenge is not trivial, it is not as difficult as developing entrepreneurs.[7] Venture capitalists are buying rather than developing entrepreneurial talent. They are doing what is widely referred to as "picking winners."

This approach is effective with the right entrepreneurs, whose opportunities are ready to be exploited and captured. It favors quick returns rather than patient capital. It specifically excludes entrepreneurs who might require more effort or time to produce results. This focus on capturing opportunities assumes a continuous supply of highly skilled entrepreneurs in which to invest, but it takes no role or responsibility for developing them.[8] It ignores the issue entirely.

The ability to pick winners, to invest in the capture of opportunities, depends on a supply of highly skilled entrepreneurs. Entrepreneurs are the origin of wealth; they are the engines and drivers of economic development. This explains why 7/8ths of the productivity increases of the U.S. economy over the last century (as measured in constant dollars) can only be accounted for by new knowledge generated by innovators and entrepreneurs. This development is not attributable to increases in any of the existing factors of production, such as land, labor, or capital.[9]

From the community's perspective, an exclusive focus on capturing opportunities is simply not sustainable. *The critical determinant of a community's economic vitality is the quantity and quality of its entrepreneurs and how well they are matched to the market opportunities they pursue. If a community fails to develop entrepreneurs, its economy will lose its power and stagnate.*

A functioning economy requires investments in capturing opportunities as well as investments in developing entrepreneurs. Both are value-adding activities in the Pipeline cycle, and, since one can't exist without the other, they naturally complement each other. Not only does the rate at which these investments are producing results have to be in balance, but the Pipeline segments in which they are working must be connected to insure a smooth and uninterrupted flow between them. These results cannot simply be expected; they must be intentionally produced with the proper control of activities and resources. This Pipeline management principle calls on communities to methodically develop entrepreneurs, not merely pick winners.

Entrepreneurs must be developed, due to the primacy of their role in the creation of wealth and the development or transformation of an economy. But because investing in entrepreneurs is less tangible than investing in specific opportunities, it gets short shrift. The processes and markets for investing in human capital are much less sophisticated than those for financial capital. If we are to be able to successfully encourage greater investment in this area, we will have to develop new instruments and mechanisms for doing so. This is an area in need of innovation.

Over the last 15 years, a great deal of energy and resources have been focused on designing systems and tools to optimize the process by which opportunities are generated, refined, implemented, managed, and harvested. These include events like business plan competitions and idea tournaments, as well as idea management software platforms. These tools and mechanisms focus on the needs of the opportunity or business, not those of the entrepreneur. Their focus is exclusively on the horizontal dimension of the Pipeline—the life cycle of the business.

This leads us to wonder, what would a system look like if it were designed to solely optimize the process by which entrepreneurs are developed, independently of the business? What kind of changes would be required if we had an exclusive focus on the vertical dimension of the Pipeline—the Skill Ladder?

One of the changes would have to be in our thinking. Individuals that focus on capturing opportunities generally believe that opportunities have an existence independent of the entrepreneur. To them, opportunities are entities that entrepreneurs find already out there in the world. They see entrepreneurship as a discovery process.

An alternative way of thinking about entrepreneurship is best represented by Saras Sarasvathy, an entrepreneurship scholar, who suggests that we need to "re-conceptualize opportunities as outcomes of, rather than precursors to, entrepreneurship. . . . I would like to argue instead that entrepreneurial opportunities are predominantly the result of people acting in entrepreneurial ways, which includes acting upon perceived opportunities. So what does it mean to act entrepreneurially? In a nutshell, acting entrepreneurially involves acting as though we create our world and our opportunities rather than discover them."[10]

Sarasvathy argues that this shift in thinking about entrepreneurship and opportunities has major implications for economic development.

> Development efforts based on the premise that entrepreneurs go where economic opportunities are look very different from efforts based on the premise that opportunities get created where the entrepreneurs are. In the former case, we invest in creating opportunities—that is, we deploy our resources toward bringing the latest technologies and the required infrastructure to the regions we are interested in developing. In other words, we invest in incentives and inducements for attracting high-tech entrepreneurs by trying to create opportunities for them locally, say, through a bio-tech incubator. . . . If instead we accepted the premise that entrepreneurs create economic opportunities, we would invest our development resources in entrepreneurship education and support local entrepreneurs who seek to leverage local resources to create

opportunities that do not depend upon technologies transplanted from other regions of the world.[11]

Systems that optimize opportunities operate very differently from systems that optimize the development of entrepreneurial skills. We need to establish a system for investing in entrepreneurs and then work to effectively integrate both into a balanced, multidimensional approach. The Pipeline helps us visualize and represent this issue, but achieving success will require us to coordinate our economic development efforts, so that our opportunity development and entrepreneur development activities are seamless, transparent, and mutually reinforcing.

Filling a Missing Function

It is fair to say that, presently, no organization is truly responsible for the quantity and the quality of the supply of entrepreneurs and enterprises in our communities. Current economic development programs only deal with part of the equation for success; they address the needs firms have for technical and financial assistance but do little to build a pipeline of highly skilled entrepreneurs capable of using that assistance effectively to build companies. What is missing is any systematic effort to *create* qualified customers for enterprise development services.

The function of developing entrepreneurs is transformational, rather than transactional, in nature. It involves work that is long-term and developmental. As a result, it cannot be the responsibility of any of the existing service provider organizations. This function must be the role of a new entity that bears responsibility for enterprise development at the community-wide level. This responsibility is too important and too challenging to be left to chance.[12]

2. Build a Community of Entrepreneurs

Earlier in the book, we defined entrepreneurs as individuals who create value or wealth by identifying and capturing market opportunities. Before we describe what we mean by an "entrepreneurial community," we would like to revisit that former definition in light of the Pipeline.

Revisiting Our Definition of an Entrepreneur

Much has been made in the business press and the entrepreneurship literature about the difference between a small business owner and an entrepreneur. In our opinion, *an entrepreneur is anyone who is seeking to move themselves and their business to another segment of the Pipeline from the one they are in.* A business owner, small or large, is anyone who is comfortable in the segment they occupy and desires to stay there. Being a businessperson is about stability and maintaining the status quo. Entrepreneurship is about transforming one's skills and one's business.

This definition does several things. First, it is inclusive of all parts of the Pipeline. Second, it recognizes that entrepreneurship is about choice and action. An entrepreneur can decide to become a businessperson and a businessperson can decide to become an entrepreneur. This ability is reflected in the choice of an entrepreneur to slow her business down for a year or two until her daughter has finished high school, in order to spend precious time with her before she leaves home; or to take care of an ailing parent. Then, once circumstances change, she chooses to aggressively move forward with her business. Individuals make choices and change them frequently over the course of their lives.

Third, it helps demonstrate how differences between these two economic roles correspond to the differences between the functions of growth and development. Businesspeople are capable of growth, which means they can improve their performance within a particular segment of the Pipeline. Entrepreneurs are capable of development, which means that they are able to transform themselves as well as their businesses and move from one segment of the Pipeline to another.

There are some whose definition of an entrepreneur is narrow and exclusive. For example, it has been argued that the only "real" entrepreneurs are those individuals with a masters degree in engineering and with an offering capable of being protected as intellectual property. We believe such attitudes are insulting and self-defeating. They fail to recognize the contribution to our economy made by other kinds of entrepreneurs. We have been in the room when individuals were told that they were not "real" entrepreneurs. What we believe these critics meant to say, and should have said, is that "you are not the kind of entrepreneur in which we invest."

There is no doubt that a game is being played. But it is a game with unhealthy consequences for our economy, no matter what explanations are offered for this behavior. The judgments we make about entrepreneurs must be functional and constructive, not stereotypical and dismissive. This is not because there should be more civility in our world, although that is certainly true, but because our judgments are leading us to waste valuable opportunities and human resources.

Too often, entrepreneurs are being seen through the wrong set of eyes. It is important to differentiate or segment entrepreneurs, but to do so meaningfully. We need a more inclusive notion of who is an entrepreneur, because we *must recognize that the economy requires all kinds of entrepreneurs and all kinds of businesses.*

We can't have an economy that consists entirely of break-through innovators or major league entrepreneurs like Gates, Jobs, Dell, Ford, and Rockefeller. We also need firms led by bureaucrats with limited creativity and entrepreneurial skills, a fact that the Enron disaster has clearly demonstrated. Focusing exclusively on one type of entrepreneur is the equivalent of suggesting that we field an entire team of quarterbacks because, as the most important position, it is the only one that matters. That begs the question, who is going to catch the ball, block, or take a handoff?

An expansive, more inclusive definition of an entrepreneur enables us to broaden the notion of who is a member of our community of entrepreneurs. It also enables those responsible for economic development to pursue overlooked opportunities to expand the scope and application of economic development strategies. By defining entrepreneurial assets more broadly, the client base can be expanded to include aspiring entrepreneurs, potential entrepreneurs, intrapreneurs working within existing companies, leaders of strategic alliances between companies, owners of declining firms who desire to reinvent or sell their business, and existing companies who want to grow through new product development or product extensions.

None of these definitions eliminate the need to make a judgment about who is worthy of attention and resources. That has to be determined on a case-by-case basis. But we can make higher-quality decisions because we have a better map.

What Is an Entrepreneurial Community?

An entrepreneurial community is a critical mass of entrepreneurs that constitutes a distinct and recognizable community within a larger community or region. This group, characterized by a network of relationships through which support, resources, know-how, and business passes, provides its members with the conditions necessary to grow their firms. These relationships give the community a sense of identity and cohesion.

Much has been written about entrepreneurial networks, their organization, and their benefits.[13] There are numerous models out there upon which to pattern a community of entrepreneurs. However, we are advocating an organization that goes well beyond information exchanges.

Entrepreneurs need to organize themselves into a community of entrepreneurs. The behavior this requires may not come naturally to many who do not considered themselves to be joiners. It will require leadership on the part of one, or a few, individuals who are willing to do the organizing in the beginning, until the group is large and stable enough to select its own leadership. Every community—rural or urban, large or small, wealthy or poor—should have such a collaboration.

3. Have Entrepreneurs Lead the Way

The changes suggested in this book will not come about without the strong support and indeed leadership of entrepreneurs. Entrepreneurs know what they need, they have skin in the game, and they have the skills necessary to implement innovative solutions.

We are talking about entrepreneurs, not business executives. The boards of most economic development organizations are filled with CEOs of hospitals, utilities, banks, insurance companies, universities, accountancies, and law firms, and with individuals who have inherited their businesses—almost none of whom have ever started or grown a business through the skill levels and business stages described in this book. As a result, they do not understand the very customers they are supposed to be helping.

The implementation of this principle will require a partnership between two very different types of professionals—traditional economic development practitioners and entrepreneurs. Both groups will pull each other out of their comfort zones, but this interaction will be very important to achieving successful outcomes. Another challenge is that entrepreneurs who are operating businesses do not have much time for anything else.[14] For this reason, we call upon entrepreneurs with mature businesses that they themselves have built, or retired entrepreneurs with available time, to step up and help develop new entrepreneurs.

Entrepreneurs need to undertake the following activities within their communities or regions:

1. Heighten the visibility of entrepreneurs and entrepreneurship and the public's awareness of their contributions to the economy and to local quality of life.

2. Educate federal, state, and local policymakers as to the value of entrepreneurship as an approach to economic development.
3. Lobby government administrators and legislators to adopt the Pipeline model of economic development.
4. Pursue leadership roles in local or regional economic development, offering to work closely with economic developers and government officials to create and implement programs that truly benefit entrepreneurs.
5. Write articles and op-ed. pieces for local newspapers that champion entrepreneurship and systemic, systematic, and strategic economic development.

Without this kind of direct action by entrepreneurs, it will be very difficult to put these positive changes in place.

4. Manage the Pipeline of Entrepreneurs and Enterprises as a Portfolio of Related Assets

The Pipeline must be managed as a system, in which the whole is greater than the sum of the parts. This is the ultimate form of economic leverage. In order to achieve this objective, we must manage not only the individual assets for which we are responsible, but the relationships among them as well.[15] These assets include the community's human capital, as well as the physical and financial capital that are contained within businesses.

This principle calls on us to attend to the health of the entire Pipeline. We must build a Pipeline in which everyone can participate. Different community members and stakeholder groups have a stronger interest in certain parts of the Pipeline than others. Government agencies are interested in both businesses and jobs as a tax base and a way to create wealth as well as provide a pathway out of poverty. Many foundations are similarly interested in encouraging entrepreneurship among youth and disadvantaged populations. Local businesses and financial institutions are interested in customers, large corporations in suppliers, educational institutions in students, and venture capitalists in deal flow. But all these stakeholders must realize that without a complete pipeline, each party's ability to have their needs met is severely compromised. Only by having a complete system can everyone get what they need.

Community leaders must avoid the trap of focusing exclusively on any single segment, with one carefully articulated exception. At any given point in time, the community may choose to allocate its limited resources in a way that favors one segment of the pipeline. As long as this choice is strategic—one that takes advantage of particular market opportunities available at the time, which is in the interest of the entire community—and not a permanent bias in the system—the decision would be equitable.[16]

Resources must be directed toward connecting the segments of the Pipeline to insure a continuous flow. The bifurcation that exists in many Pipelines between the Zone of Potential and the Zone of Maximization must be overcome. In addition, local economies will benefit from being part of a larger region, as long as the resources are distributed effectively and equitably.

Pipeline managers must look for opportunities to produce multiplier effects—of both an economic and developmental nature. Economic multipliers refer to the number of times a dollar will circulate in the community. The greater the number of linkages among local businesses, the larger the multiplier effect will be. Developmental multipliers refer to the social linkages that exist among entrepreneurs and the influence that travels along those channels. The presence of role models as well as supportive peers will promote the flow of learning, inspiration, and positive norms of behavior. Similarly, the greater the social capital, the larger the multiplier effect will be. Both kinds of linkages will be crucial to transforming the economy.

Additionally, community leaders must:

- Pursue a variety of strategies designed to improve the volume and the flows throughout the Pipeline.
- Stick to their strategy regardless of passing fads. This is one of Warren Buffet's investment principles.
- Experiment freely and, at the same time, make an effort to limit the downside risk of failure. "The key issue is not avoiding failure, but managing the cost of failure by limiting exposure to the downside while preserving access to attractive opportunities and maximizing gains. A high failure rate can even be positive, provided that the cost of failing is bounded. For instance, 'churn' (high rates of business founding and exiting) is associated with economic vibrancy."[17]
- Coordinate strategies to insure that the movement in the pipeline is smooth and sustainable. Operate with a surgeon's precision and carefully sequence strategies over time. Start with low-hanging fruit

(undervalued assets with high margin potential), but quickly stretch to incubating strategies that sustain the flow of entrepreneurs and enterprises.

- Be creative about defining human assets. Seek out overlooked individuals in our communities.[18]
- Take the long view when developing entrepreneurs. Invest capital with patience.

By managing the Pipeline as a portfolio of related assets made up of entrepreneurs and enterprises, community leaders will be able to transform their economy.

5. Operate in a Client-Centered Manner

Most enterprise development activities are driven by the use of a particular tool, rather than by meeting a particular entrepreneurial need. In other words, they are supply- rather than demand-driven. The focus needs to shift from the tools to the clients. Strategies must be grounded in a Pipeline analysis, with attention to the criteria of efficiency, effectiveness, equity, sustainability, and scale. Efforts will have to be made to determine how various strategies can be integrated to create a recipe that will help transform the economy. This orientation will make individual economic development strategies more relevant by deploying them in a more effective manner, at the right times, and under the right conditions.

6. Invest in the Conditions Necessary to Effectively Manage the Pipeline of Entrepreneurs and Enterprises

Making the investments necessary to manage the pipeline is crucial. The right infrastructure can produce a significant improvement in the probabilities of success for everyone in the community.[19] If designed and implemented properly up front (with sufficient and appropriate funding to perform the necessary functions), the results can be systemic, systematic, and strategic as opposed to ad hoc; and the returns would be extraordinarily positive. The objective is to set the right conditions in place, so that the ongoing cost of operating the system and producing favorable outcomes is marginal.

By contrast, our current approach to economic development is highly fragmented and piecemeal.[20] The patchwork of existing activities is often incomplete and incompatible, rarely functioning as a system. The results, from the community's perspective, are often ineffective, inefficient, inequitable, unsustainable, and lacking in scale.

We believe that, in many cases, the demand for self-sufficiency on the part of enterprise development programs is a direct attempt to dodge responsibility for managing the Pipeline. Most low-skilled entrepreneurs and early-stage enterprises are not in a position to pay for assistance. Does that mean that it is not in the community's interest to help them and that we should not provide them with support? We do not ask children to pay the costs of their education until they are old enough and capable enough to do so. That is the role of parents—to incubate their children. These are investments, not subsidies, and must be made under terms that are consistent with that approach.

Similarly, the public sector does play a role in incubating new businesses—one that is frequently unrecognized. Silicon Valley, the epitome of a successful economic region, was itself incubated by huge public investments in technology by the U.S. Department of Defense. Notwithstanding their claims, the rewards being reaped by venture capitalists in that region are a direct consequence, not the cause, of the seeds planted by public investment.

The scale of investment in the Pipeline and its duration must be sufficient to meet the community's needs. We are often asked how long a region or community must continue to invest in its Pipeline. Once we were making a presentation to a crowd from Michigan during a year when the Detroit Tigers were playing in the World Series for the baseball championship title. When this question came up, we responded with a simple question in return: if the Tigers win the World Series, will you then be willing to dismantle your farm system? The audience responded with an audible gasp, indicating how shocked they were by such a question—to even suggest such a thing. But they were more than ready to suspend an investment in the Pipeline at the first sign that positive things were happening.

Communities must continue to invest in their economic development, particularly in good economic times, so that the investment bears fruit during economic downturns. Many communities are engaged in "triage" operations, only because they failed to function in a methodical and proactive way that would enable them to at least anticipate, if not avoid, emergencies and crisis management. As Clayton Christensen of Harvard University points out, "It isn't possible to manage growth in the same way [as driving a car]—to wait until the growth gauge begins falling toward zero before you seek a fill-up from new growth businesses. The growth engine is a much more delicate machine that must be kept running continuously by process and policy, rather than by reacting when the growth gauge reads empty."[21] A well-planned process will provide a community with greater options, more time, and the ability to respond proactively and with sensitivity to the needs of its citizens.

7. Reconceptualize the Role of Economic Developers as Change Agents

In order to operate in the manner suggested by these Pipeline principles, the roles and responsibilities of economic development practitioners need to be reconceptualized. Working with entrepreneurs is not the same as providing affordable housing, for example. Enterprise development efforts cannot be run like social service agencies. There is a base of business knowledge and experience without which one cannot function competently, and a range of skills that must be possessed to be an effective agent of change.

Economic developers need to be accountable for producing results, not vision statements. As Thomas Edison observed, "vision without execution is hallucination." No more prizes should be awarded for forecasting rain, only for building the ark. From our long experience in the business incubation industry, we are all too familiar with the fact that governments are willing to spend millions of dollars to renovate an old building as an incubator, but rarely more than $25,000 a year to operate the program designed to help entrepreneurs. These priorities must be reversed. We must stop focusing on appearances and instead concentrate on performance.

There will be resistance to these changes, as well as to the adoption of the Pipeline and its underlying philosophy.[22] As Everett Rogers has described, some will be "early adopters," but a majority will be much harder to convince. Some will be "laggards" who will only come along kicking and screaming.[23] Patience and tenacity will be required to make the change.

The Pipeline approach seeks to supplant the reigning model of economic development, with its focus on big business and business attraction and retention activities. In other words, it threatens to disrupt business as usual. Nevertheless, as entrepreneurs know, disruptions are not necessarily a bad thing. They can lead to increased efficiency and effectiveness. Some activities will fall by the wayside because they are obsolete or ineffectual. This is as it should be. But it should be emphasized that the Pipeline itself is not intended to replace other strategies and tools of economic development; rather, it aims to refocus those strategies and tools to permit their more strategic deployment. In this way, it is more complementary than competitive.

Innovations that require new skills in order to implement them are often perceived as threats. People fear that they may not possess, or be able to learn, the new requisite skill set. Without doubt, the entrepreneurship-based Pipeline approach will require new skills, but anyone can be trained in effectively using it.

Another challenge facing the implementation of the Pipeline is the tendency in the enterprise development arena to focus on the system at the expense of the individual, and almost never on both. Most public policy approaches to fostering entrepreneurship are aimed at creating the context, or the system. Some seek to create a "culture of entrepreneurship" by encouraging and/or training government officials, policymakers, and others in the community to "think like entrepreneurs." Others place their focus on constructing the hard (telecommunications systems, roadways, schools) and soft (technical, financial, and social assistance) infrastructures believed to be necessary to support successful business entrepreneurship. Still others focus their attention on educating and lobbying state and federal government officials about the economic virtues of entrepreneurship in hopes of stimulating regulatory and financial support. While all of these approaches are commendable, none is complete. The problem with hovering at 20,000 feet is that one cannot see the trees for the forest. The individual entrepreneur is neglected.

This happens because many public policymakers and foundation people choose to believe that it is not their place to help private businesspeople directly (unless they are low-income individuals), and that entrepreneurs already have the innate traits it takes to succeed; they just need a supportive context within which to work. Policymakers also typically know little or nothing about how entrepreneurship truly works, and, therefore, they avoid its actual practice. Furthermore, policymakers believe that the myriad entrepreneurship programs in existence are up to the task of helping individual entrepreneurs; so, in their minds, they've got that aspect covered.

The problem with this perspective is that it is based on false perceptions. First, we now know that entrepreneurs are made, not born.[24] They must master skill sets in order to be successful, which suggests they can be helped to develop faster than they might if left to their own devices.[25] Thus, merely creating entrepreneurship-friendly contexts is not enough. Building entrepreneurship skills is essential.

A growing body of research is finding that existing enterprise development organizations are not up to the task of developing the skills of entrepreneurs.[26] This is due to a host of reasons, not the least of which is the fact that these organizations lack the depth and breadth of business experience and skill necessary.[27] If entrepreneurs are not born to their calling, and current assistance lacks the capability to be genuinely useful, where does that leave the individual entrepreneur and her company? Any effort to foster entrepreneurship must address the system *and* the individual, if it hopes to ultimately be successful.

Communities must evaluate the costs of not changing. Like entrepreneurs, communities face competitive risks: the risk of losing entrepreneurs, people, jobs, and assets to other communities, regions, and nations. No longer does the city down the highway represent the competition in this global economy. We can no longer be complacent about how much time we have to make these changes, either. Politicians and community leaders often act as if they have all the time in the world, but businesses do not respond to political timeframes. While communities stand still to debate their future, the world is moving forward.

Economic developers can be leaders of this change. They can advocate for entrepreneur-centered economic development. They can be Pipeline innovators and early adopters. They can work with entrepreneurs to identify and implement viable strategies for their communities. They can build their own skill sets relative to the development of entrepreneurs and their businesses. They can do all of these things, if they will accept the challenge.

CONCLUSION

If the Pipeline is to be used effectively, it must be carefully managed according to the principles enunciated in this chapter. This strategic management process begins with placing the focus on the community's entrepreneurs—being entrepreneur-centric. A commitment, in the form of an investment, must be made in developing local entrepreneurs, not just developing opportunities for them. The entrepreneurs should coalesce into a community that has the power to highlight their contributions to the local economy and quality of life, to advocate for their needs, and to give them a place at the table as the community maps its strategy for economic transformation. Entrepreneurs should play leadership roles in the implementation of this strategy.

The community's entrepreneurs and enterprises should be treated as a portfolio of related business assets and managed accordingly. This requires that economic developers approach managing their Pipelines holistically and link all segments together, not favoring certain segments over others. Economic development strategies should be targeted to specific needs, goals, and parts of the Pipeline, but this should be done in a way that sustains the entire Pipeline, its volume, and its flow.

Managing a community's Pipeline requires investment, not subsidy. The potential returns on this investment are enormous in terms of economic transformation. This should be investment in both hard infrastructure and soft infrastructure and should be made according to the community's needs and its goals for economic development. It should be investment that is sustained and sustainable.

Undertaking all of this activity requires a change in the way we think about economic development and the role of economic developers. Economic development that is entrepreneur-centric requires practitioners who are business-savvy themselves, and who partner with entrepreneurs to fill gaps in knowledge and expertise as they plan for and execute their strategies. Performance becomes paramount and must be measured and managed. There must be openness to continuous innovation. Economic developers must think in terms of *both* the system and the individuals in that system (i.e., the Pipeline and the entrepreneurs in the Pipeline). It is no longer enough to merely set the stage for successful entrepreneurship, assuming the individual entrepreneurs will take care of themselves. Economic developers must see themselves as *developers of entrepreneurs*.

The change is coming. Economic developers can choose to manage this change or be managed by it. We urge them to choose the former.

Conclusion

Never doubt that a small group of thoughtful, committed citizens can change the world. Indeed, it's the only thing that ever has.

—Margaret Mead

This book is about how to understand the differences among entrepreneurs and enterprises in order to support their growth and development. We present a "map" called the Pipeline, which is more than just a metaphor; it gives us a method of meaningfully segmenting our marketplace or customer base. The Pipeline helps us answer fundamental questions about who these entrepreneurs are, what they need, and how can we best help them build successful companies.

The Pipeline refocuses economic development strategies to assist entrepreneurs and entrepreneurship in a highly targeted, systemic, and systematic way. The knowledge or understanding generated by this map will enable the field of economic development to advance from being tool-driven to being client-centered.

Two key variables make up the Pipeline: entrepreneurial skills and business life cycle stages. The skill ladder represents the vertical dimension and sorts entrepreneurs into five skill levels: Rookies, Single As, Double As, Triple As, and Major Leaguers. The life cycle stages represent the horizontal dimension and sort enterprises into six phases: Pre-Venture, Existence, Early Growth, Expansion, Maturity, and Decline.

Entrepreneurs at each skill level think and behave differently from those at other levels. Each higher skill level represents a greater ability than the level below it. These differences are qualitative and significant, not incremental in nature. Movement from one skill level to another requires a transformation in the abilities of the entrepreneur—a fundamental and discontinuous change. The best way to facilitate skill building in entrepreneurs is through coaching.

These differences are also reflected in the economic performance between entrepreneurs at various skill levels, as measured by sales revenue, productivity rates, and levels of innovation. A much higher level of skill is required to achieve financial success than in the past, because increased market competition continues to raise the bar. But the importance of and return to the mastery of entrepreneurial skills continue to increase as well.

Entrepreneurs and businesses are not one and the same, and their separation in the Pipeline is crucial to the mapping process. The business is a creation of the entrepreneur, a manifestation of the entrepreneur's goals and efforts. An entrepreneur can, and in many cases will, create many different businesses over the course of her lifetime.

The development of the business is a process that takes place over time and through distinct stages. Movement from one stage to the next stage in the life cycle requires a transformation in the structure of the operations. It is a whole new game at each stage in the life cycle, as many entrepreneurs are often quite surprised to discover. Each stage makes different demands on a business. By understanding these requirements, support can be provided that is specifically targeted to those needs.

Together, the two dimensions of entrepreneurs and enterprises are assembled to form a Pipeline that enables a community or region to map its entrepreneurial assets and capture their volume and flow. This gives us a new, richer lens through which to view this marketplace, rather than the typical mass market representation of a homogenous pool of players. By coding the entrepreneurs and enterprises in the Pipeline with additional information such as industry, demographic characteristics, and performance, we can produce various maps that provide detailed knowledge about the composition of assets in the community. The Pipeline gives us the ability to look at the population of entrepreneurs in our communities or regions as a whole *and* as a set of parts, so that we can see and manage the relationship of the parts to the whole.

The Pipeline reveals several very important insights. The first is that the needs of entrepreneurs and enterprises in each segment of the Pipeline are *different*, as are the services (e.g., financing, business planning, or training) and the infrastructure necessary to support them. The second is that movement from one segment of the Pipeline to another requires a transformation—either the development of new skills or the evolution of the business to the next stage in the life cycle. The Pipeline gives us a way to illustrate and operationalize the critical differences between growth and development. Growth is an increase in the performance of an entrepreneur or enterprise *within* a particular segment of the Pipeline; it occurs without a change in structure. Development is a fundamental change or transformation in the structure of the entrepreneur's skills or enterprise's operations, which involves the movement or flow of that asset to a more advanced segment of the Pipeline.

This map helps us visualize the dynamics that occur within the Pipeline as a result of the interaction between entrepreneurial skills and the business life cycle. We see that there are various points in the Pipeline at which entrepreneurs and their businesses tend to get stuck. Also, there are stages in the life cycle to which the entrepreneur cannot successfully advance the business *unless* he first increases his skill level; otherwise, the business crashes. Some segments of the Pipeline are only reachable by an entrepreneur if they inherit or acquire a business that is beyond their skills. In such cases, they are in trouble. One of the key lessons here is that entrepreneurial success requires a match between skill levels and the requirements of the business. An entrepreneur, over the course of his career, can both increase his skill level as well as the value of his business assets by being strategic about his movements through the Pipeline.

The challenge in managing the Pipeline is how to increase both the quantity (i.e., volume) and the quality of the supply of entrepreneurs and enterprises in the community. This can be done by the appropriate utilization of various economic development strategies. These strategies can be sorted into three categories according to their impact on the Pipeline. Performance enhancement strategies are designed to improve the quality of the assets or stock within each segment of the Pipeline— to increase or accelerate growth and profitability. Incubation strategies are designed to change (i.e., transform) assets or stock by improving the flow or movement of entrepreneurs and enterprises between segments in the Pipeline. Selective attraction strategies are designed to add new players or stock to the Pipeline. These three sets of strategies can be used in every segment of the Pipeline. In order to be effective, however, the implementation of particular economic development strategies at any one point in time must be targeted to a specific part of the Pipeline, with an eye toward the health of the entire Pipeline. Performance enhancement and strategic attraction are strategies for growth, not development. Only incubation strategies produce development—by increasing the flow from one segment in the Pipeline to another.

The Pipeline can be used to diagnose critical economic challenges being faced by many regions throughout the world. It can also be used to help design strategic interventions in a way that hits their targets and achieves a measurable return-on-investment. The field of economic development must become more performance-oriented. In order to do so, performance evaluation must be built into the design and management of these initiatives, not engaged in after the fact. This can be done by "engineering" the project and clearly specifying targets and assumptions to be clarified in the process of implementation.

In order to build wealth for the community or region and transform our economies, we need to be strategic about the management of the Pipeline. There are seven principles that should guide our actions:

1. Invest in developing entrepreneurs.
2. Build a community of entrepreneurs.
3. Have entrepreneurs lead the way.
4. Manage the Pipeline of Entrepreneurs and Enterprises as a portfolio of related assets.
5. Operate in a client-centered manner.
6. Invest in the conditions necessary to effectively manage the Pipeline of Entrepreneurs and Enterprises.
7. Reconceptualize the role of economic developers as change agents.

Economic development in the 21st century should be focused on managing our regional portfolios of entrepreneurial assets across the country. In order to achieve this, we are asking people to change their current paradigm of what economic development is and how it should be pursued. We are championing a spotlight on entrepreneurship—innovation and growth through new business creation and existing business rebirth—as opposed to corporatism. We are calling for putting the "development" back into economic development and abandoning the current exclusive focus on growth. We are suggesting that this new movement should be led by entrepreneurs, rather than bureaucrats. Finally, we are advocating that this approach be systemic, systematic, and strategic, not fragmented, categorical, transactional and political.

The Pipeline of Entrepreneurs and Enterprises is an operational map that gives all of us—local business leaders, policymakers, and economic development practitioners—a framework for making informed decisions about where to invest in entrepreneurship and how to manage the community's portfolio of entrepreneurial assets.

First, the Pipeline enables us to bring this much-needed systemic, systematic, and strategic approach to economic development. It is systemic in the sense that it forces economic developers to consider the "big picture" at all times. It takes into account both development and growth. It includes all the levels and stages in the development process—for both individual entrepreneurs and their businesses—and how these dimensions interact. It is systematic in that it emphasizes the appropriate path to be followed in developing an entrepreneur as well in developing her company and enforces doing the right things in the right order. These characteristics allow economic developers to be strategic in selecting interventions that are appropriate to each segment of the Pipeline and that are complementary to and reinforcing of each other.

Second, the Pipeline ensures a strong link between the individual and the system. Skill development of individual entrepreneurs is featured. Growth and development of individual companies can be assessed and tracked. These are appropriately connected to the community- or region-wide strategies and tactics utilized to foster this growth and development. Both the individual entrepreneur and his context are considered and addressed in a way that brings them together synergistically.

Third, the Pipeline effectively segments the market of entrepreneurs and enterprises—to the benefit of both economic developers and their clients. Economic developers become more effective, providing assistance that is highly tailored to the needs of their clients and increasing the probability of success. Entrepreneurs gain from the improvement in the services they receive, enhancing their skills and the quality of their businesses.

Finally, the Pipeline model places entrepreneurship at the heart of economic development, and our innovators (entrepreneurs) in a leadership role. This brings us, as a nation, back to our roots and in a position to compete effectively in a global economy that demands constant innovation.

Notes

Introduction

1. Cortlandt Cammann, "Action Usable Knowledge," in *Exploring Clinical Methods for Social Research,* ed. David N. Berg and Kenwyn K. Smith (Beverly Hills, CA: Sage Publications, 1985), 115.

2. For more information regarding action research methods and their scientific foundations, see Chris Argyris, Robert Putnam, and Diane McLain Smith, *Action Science* (San Francisco: Jossey-Bass, 1985); P. Bourdieu, *Outline of a Theory of Practice* (Cambridge: Cambridge University Press, 1990); P. Bourdieu and L.D.C. Wacquant, *An Invitation to a Reflexive Sociology* (Chicago: University of Chicago Press, 1992); Kurt Lewin, *Field Theory in Social Science* (New York: Harpers and Brothers, 1951); D.A. Schon, *The Reflective Practitioner* (New York: Basic Books, 1983); D.A. Schon, *Educating the Reflective Practitioner* (San Francisco: Jossey-Bass, 1987); W.F. Whyte, "On the Uses of Social Science Research," *American Sociological Review* 51 (1986): 555–63; and W.F. Whyte, D.J. Greenwood, and P. Lazes, "Participatory Action Research: Through Practice to Science in Social Research," in *Participatory Action Research,* ed. W.F. Whyte, 19–55 (Newbury Park, CA: Sage, 1991).

3. "American men have a naughty little secret. Sometimes, they like to relax with a little Céline Dion. Professed classical music fans have one, too: as it turns out, they don't tune into classical radio nearly as much as they claim. These are two of many findings shaking up the radio industry as it converts from measuring ratings through surveys to monitoring listeners electronically using so-called Portable People Meters." See Stephanie Clifford, "Never Listen to Céline? Radio Meter Begs to Differ," *New York Times*, December 16, 2009.

4. G.A. Lichtenstein, T.S. Lyons, and N. Kutzhanova, "Building Entrepreneurial Communities: The Appropriate Role of Enterprise Development Activities," *Journal of the Community Development Society* 35, no. 1 (2004): 11.

5. For a good discussion of this issue, see Lichtenstein, Lyons, and Kut-zhanova, "Building Entrepreneurial Communities."

6. J. H. Gilmore and B. J. Pine II, "Beyond Goods and Services," *Strategy & Leadership,* May/June 1997, 14.

7. Ibid., 13.

8. Ibid., 14.

9. Ibid.

10. See Gregg A. Lichtenstein, "The Significance of Relationships in Entre-preneurship: A Case Study of the Ecology of Enterprise in Two Business Incu-bators" (Ph.D. dissertation, University of Pennsylvania, 1992).

11. See Gregg A. Lichtenstein and Thomas S. Lyons, "Revisiting the Busi-ness Life-Cycle: Proposing an Actionable Model for Assessing and Fostering Entrepreneurship," *International Journal of Entrepreneurship and Innovation* 9, no. 4 (2008): 241–50.

Chapter 1

1. Joseph A. Schumpeter, *The Theory of Economic Development* (New Bruns-wick, NJ: Transaction Publishers, 1983).

2. D. Pozen, "We Are All Entrepreneurs Now," *Wake Forest Law Review* 43, no. 1 (2008).

3. Burton H. Klein, *Dynamic Economics* (Cambridge, MA: Harvard Uni-versity Press, 1977), 9.

4. We are often asked to distinguish between entrepreneurship and self-employment. Our response is to point out that, unlike the self-employed, an entrepreneur is an innovator who has a goal of growth for his or her business. This is also compatible with Klein's definition. We use the term *innovator* in its broadest sense. Innovation does not merely include the invention of totally new products or services. It also embraces finding new markets for and/or adding value to existing products and services. See Schumpeter, *The Theory of Economic Development,* and J. G. Longenecker, C. W. Moore, J. W. Petty, and L. E. Palich, *Small Business Management: An Entrepreneurial Emphasis,* 13th ed. (Mason, OH: Thomson South-Western, 2006).

5. Kenryu Hashikawa, "Rural Entrepreneurship in New Jersey during the Early Republic," Ph.D. diss., Columbia University, 2002.

6. Gerald Gunderson, *The Wealth Creators: An Entrepreneurial History of the United States* (New York: Penguin Books, 1990).

7. Ibid., 25.

8. See Gunderson, *The Wealth Creators,* 1990.

9. G. Heberton Evans Jr., "A Century of Entrepreneurship in the United States with Emphases upon Large Manufacturing Concerns," *Explorations in Entrepreneurial History* 10, no. 2 (1957): 90–103.

10. Sam Bass Warner Jr., *The Private City: Philadelphia in Three Periods of Its Growth,* 2nd ed. (Philadelphia: University of Pennsylvania Press, 1987).

11. J. A. Timmons and S. Spinelli, *New Venture Creation: Entrepreneurship for the 21st Century* (Boston: McGraw-Hill Irwin, 2007), 51.

12. R.E. Hamlin and T.S. Lyons, *Financing Small Business in America: Debt Capital in the Global Economy* (Westport, CT: Praeger, 2003), 5.

13. Timmons and Spinelli, *New Venture Creation*, 51.

14. Hamlin and Lyons, *Financing Small Business in America*, 5.

15. G.A. Lichtenstein and T.S. Lyons, "Managing the Community's Pipeline of Entrepreneurs and Enterprises: A New Way of Thinking about Business Assets," *Economic Development Quarterly* 20, no. 4 (2006): 377–86.

Chapter 2

1. G.A. Lichtenstein and T.S Lyons, "The Entrepreneurial Development System: Transforming Business Talent and Community Economies," *Economic Development Quarterly* 15, no. 1 (2001): 3–20.

2. See G.A. Lichtenstein, T.S Lyons, and N. Kutzhanova, "Building Entrepreneurial Communities: The Appropriate Role of Enterprise Development Activities," *Journal of the Community Development Society* 35, no. 1 (2004): 5–24.

3. C. Henry, F. Hill, and C. Leitch, "Developing a Coherent Enterprise Support Policy: A New Challenge for Government," *Planning and Environment C: Government and Policy* 21, no. 1 (2003): 3–19.

4. The Center for Rural Entrepreneurship has recently made a step in this direction with the initiation of a program to work directly with entrepreneurs in rural communities.

5. See G.A. Lichtenstein and T.S Lyons, *Incubating New Enterprises* (Washington, DC: The Aspen Institute, 1996).

6. D. DeFaoite, C. Henry, K. Johnston, and P. van der Sijde, "Education and Training for Entrepreneurs: A Consideration of Initiatives in Ireland and the Netherlands," *Education and Training* 45, nos. 8–9 (2003): 430–38.

7. Lichtenstein and Lyons, "The Entrepreneurial Development System."

8. J.A. Timmons and S. Spinelli, *New Venture Creation: Entrepreneurship for the 21st Century* (Boston, MA: McGraw-Hill Irwin, 2007).

Chapter 3

1. Grant Godwin, from Martin Marietta Composites in North Carolina.

2. See T.M. Begley and D.P. Boyd, "Psychological Characteristics Associated with Performance in Entrepreneurial Firms and Smaller Businesses," *Journal of Business Venturing* 2, no. 1 (1987): 79–93; J.A. Hornaday and J. Aboud, "Characteristics of Successful Entrepreneurs," *Personnel Psychology* 24 (1971): 141–53; D.C. McClelland, J.W. Atkinson, R.A. Clark, and E.L. Lowell, *The Achievement Motive* (New York: Appleton-Century-Crofts, 1953); A. Rauch and M. Frese, "Psychological Approaches to Entrepreneurial Success: A General Model and an Overview of Findings," in *International Review of Industrial and Organizational Psychology*, ed. C.L. Cooper and I.T. Robertson (Chichester, Sussex, UK: Wiley & Sons, 2000); R.H. Brockhaus Sr., "Risk Taking Propensity

of Entrepreneurs," *Academy of Management Journal* 23 (1980): 509–20; J. B. Rotter, "Generalized Expectancies for Internal versus External Control of Reinforcement," *Psychological Monographs* 80, no. 1 (1966): 1–28; R. H. Brockhaus Sr. and P.S. Horwitz, "The Psychology of the Entrepreneur," in *The Art and Science of Entrepreneurship*, ed. D. L. Sexton and R. W. Smilor, 25–48 (Cambridge, MA: Ballinger, 1986); D. L. Hull, J. J. Bosley, and G. G. Udell, "Renewing the Hunt for the Heffalump: Identifying Potential Entrepreneurs by Personality Characteristics," *Journal of Business Management* 20, no. 2 (1982): 11–19; J. Timmons, L. Smollen, and A. Dingee, *New Venture Creation: A Guide to Entrepreneurship* (Hamate, IL: Irwin, 1985); S. K. Kassicieh, H. R. Radosevich, and C. M. Banbury. "Using Attitudinal, Situational, and Personal Characteristics Variables to Predict Future Entrepreneurs from National Laboratory Inventors," *IEEE Transactions on Engineering Management* 44 (1997): 248–57; A. C. Cooper and W. C. Dunkelberg, "Entrepreneurial Research: Old Questions, New Answers, and Methodological Issues," *American Journal of Small Business* 11, no. 3 (1987): 1–20.

3. This statement assumes that an individual is ready, willing, and able to do the work necessary to become a skilled entrepreneur, as described in more detail later in this chapter.

4. Robert Kegan and Lisa Laskow Lahey, *Immunity to Change* (Cambridge, MA: Harvard Business Press, 2009), 11.

5. Anne Midgette, "The End of the Great Big American Voice," *New York Times*, November 13, 2005.

6. See G. A. Lichtenstein and T. S. Lyons, *Incubating New Enterprises: A Guide to Successful Practice* (Washington, DC: The Aspen Institute, 1996).

7. See M. E. Gerber, *The E-Myth Revisited: Why Most Small Businesses Don't Work and What to Do About It* (New York: HarperCollins, 1995) for an excellent description of an entrepreneur operating at this skill level.

8. Data provided by the Major League Baseball Players Association, http://mlbplayers.mlb.com/pa/index.jsp.

9. Source: Globalsecurity.org, http://www.globalsecurity.org/military/intro/ranks.htm, as of November 30, 2004.

10. See Daniel Goleman, *Emotional Intelligence* (New York: Bantam Books, 1995).

11. For example, coaching will only be effective if clients have the personal maturity to listen and learn from others—their peers, their coach, and other, more experienced entrepreneurs who can serve as role models.

12. A corporate CEO is not necessarily a Major League entrepreneur. In fact, rarely is that the case, except in the previously mentioned example. But if large corporations are to be able to sustain their success and grow over time, they will have to develop and manage systems that facilitate entrepreneurship in their companies.

13. We are often asked how anyone who behaves in this manner can be in business, but one would be amazed at how many business owners operate at this level and their businesses still exist (although barely). One would also be surprised at the high level of intelligence and, in some cases, the educational background of these individuals. Again, it is not how smart you are that determines your skill level; it is your level of thinking and behavior. As we will

discuss in more detail in a later chapter, there are a large number of Rookies operating businesses in every community.

14. Boris Zlotin and Alla Zusman, "Levels of Invention and Intellectual Property Strategies," unpublished paper, Southfield, Michigan, Ideation International, December 2003, 6–7.

15. The Entrepreneurial League System® (ELS) is an innovative approach to identifying and developing entrepreneurial talent. The ELS is designed to help entrepreneurs grow their businesses by developing their skill. We organize individual entrepreneurs into teams according to their skill in creating or growing a business—Rookies, Single A, Double A, and Triple A. Entrepreneurs work intensively with performance coaches who are themselves skilled entrepreneurs, in weekly one-on-one sessions, monthly team meetings with their peers, and triannual large group sessions among entrepreneurs from other teams and at other skills levels. The Entrepreneurial League System® generates an ongoing supply of highly skilled entrepreneurs capable of building successful companies in sufficient numbers to transform a region's economy and create individual as well as community wealth. For more information about the ELS visit http://www.entreleaguesystem.com.

16. In 2005, our community client was one of six organizations out of a total of 183 applicants across the United States to receive a $2 million W. K. Kellogg Foundation grant (from a special 75th anniversary Request for Proposals) to expand their implementation of the Entrepreneurial League System®.

17. This project is being operated as a joint venture between Collaborative Strategies, LLC (which owns the Entrepreneurial League System®) and Cenla Advantage Partnership, a regional nonprofit focused on economic development.

18. William R. Torbert, *The Balance of Power, Transforming Self, Society, and Scientific Inquiry* (Newbury Park, CA: Sage Publications, 1991), 55.

19. Ibid., Table 3.1, 56.

20. Ibid.

21. Peter A. Corning, *Holistic Darwinism* (Chicago: University of Chicago Press, 2005), 119.

22. Ibid.

23. In several situations, social investors (i.e., foundations, government agencies, and other nonprofits) were considering making an investment in the Entrepreneurial League System®, which is based on the Skill Ladder presented here. Because the investors had no personal experience as entrepreneurs and felt that they could not fairly judge the value of these distinctions or the program offering, we were asked to make a presentation directly to entrepreneurs. In each case, all of the entrepreneurs stated that the distinctions were valid and that they could see themselves—where they are currently as well as where they have been (for those that have advanced up the ladder) in this framework.

24. Geoff Colvin, *Talent Is Overrated* (New York: The Penguin Group, 2008), 15.

25. Burton H. Klein, *Prices, Wages and Business Cycles: A Dynamic Theory* (Elmsford, NY: Pergamon Press, 1984), 5.

26. See Colvin, *Talent Is Overrated,* and Daniel Coyle, *The Talent Code* (New York: Bantam, 2009).

27. Coyle, *The Talent Code*, 53.

28. See Malcolm Gladwell, *Outliers* (New York: Little, Brown and Company, 2008).

29. Ibid.

30. Rita Gunther McGrath and Ian C. MacMillan, *Discovery-Driven Growth* (Cambridge, MA: Harvard Business Press. 2009), 53.

31. See P. Burrows and J. Greene, "Yes, Steve, You Fixed It. Congrats! Now What's Act Two?" *BusinessWeek*, July 31, 2000, cover story.

32. Coyle, *The Talent Code*, 32.

33. Ibid., 52.

34. Providing services is not the same as developing entrepreneurs. Services do not create a change in capacity.

35. GEM is a not-for-profit academic research consortium that has as its goal making high-quality international research data on entrepreneurial activity readily available to as wide an audience as possible.

36. Coyle, *The Talent Code*, 101.

37. J.E.A. Autere, "Is Entrepreneurship Learned? Influence of Mental Models on Growth Motivation, Strategy, and Growth," Working Paper Series 2000/7, Espo, Finland: Institute of Strategy and International Business.

Chapter 4

1. See Gregg A. Lichtenstein and Thomas S. Lyons, "Revisiting the Business Life-Cycle: Proposing an Actionable Model for Assessing and Fostering Entrepreneurship," *International Journal of Entrepreneurship and Innovation* 9, no. 4 (2008): 241–50 for a full treatment of this subject.

2. The authors have developed a detailed assessment tool to determine the life cycle stage of a business.

3. G. A. Lichtenstein and T. S. Lyons, "Managing the Community's Pipeline of Entrepreneurs and Enterprises: A New Way of Thinking about Business Assets," *Economic Development Quarterly* 20, no. 4 (2006), 379–80.

4. Burton H. Klein, *Prices, Wages and Business Cycles: A Dynamic Theory* (Elmsford, NY: Pergamon Press, 1984), 3.

5. G. A. Moore, *Dealing with Darwin* (New York: Penguin Group, 2005), xix.

6. J. Case, "A Study of Gazelles by Cognetics," *Inc. Magazine*, May 2001, 28–29.

7. See Lichtenstein and Lyons, "Revisiting the Business Life-Cycle."

Chapter 5

1. Jan L. Souman, Ilja Frissen, Manish N. Sreenivasa, and Marc O. Ernst, "Walking Straight into Circles," *Current Biology* 19, no. 18 (2009): 1538–42.

2. A pool is a flat surface without any reference points for establishing position and direction.

3. Edwin A. Abbott, *Flatland: Romance of Many Dimensions,* 5th ed. (New York: HarperCollins, 1963).

4. A highly developed system of measuring business performance would involve creating measures that are specific to each life cycle stage, since their performance requirements are quite different. For example, in addition to measures such as jobs, revenue, and profitability, this system would include measurements of assets and wealth creation effects beyond job income.

5. Kevin Morgan, "The Exaggerated Death of Geography: Learning, Proximity and Territorial Innovation Systems," *Journal of Economic Geography* 4 (2004): 17–18.

6. It is difficult to get accurate figures for entrepreneurs below the Double A skill level.

7. It is useful to think of the current situation as reflecting a "natural" flow rate, so to speak, in the absence of any attempt to change it, or at least a before-and-after difference.

8. For an analysis that maps publicly available secondary data onto the Pipeline, see Scott Loveridge and Denys Nizalov, "Operationalizing the Entrepreneurial Pipeline Theory: An Empirical Assessment of the Optimal Size Distribution of Local Firms," *Economic Development Quarterly* 21, no. 3 (2007): 244–62.

Chapter 6

1. Data assembled by *Sports Illustrated* from a host of sources (athletes, players' associations, agents, and financial advisers) indicates that by the time they have been retired for two years, 78 percent of former National Football League players have gone bankrupt or are under financial stress because of joblessness or divorce. Within five years of retirement, an estimated 60 percent of former National Basketball Association players are broke. The combination of sudden wealth and inadequate financial discipline or skill leads to trouble. This situation, known as sudden wealth syndrome, can be seen in the Internet businesses of the late 1990s that were flush with cash, property owners in Louisiana or the Middle East who found oil beneath their land, and lottery winners. See Pablo S. Torre, "How (and Why) Athletes Go Broke," *Sports Illustrated,* March 23, 2009, http://sportsillustrated.cnn.com/vault/article/maga zine/MAG1153364/index/index.htm.

2. Saras Sarasvathy, an entrepreneurship researcher and educator, noted that "studying habitual entrepreneurs, very few empirical studies have been conducted and virtually no theoretical development has taken place in this area. It is clear, however, that serial entrepreneurs account for a substantial (a third or more) of new firms in several countries." Saras D. Sarasvathy, *Effectuation: Elements of Entrepreneurial Expertise* (Northampton, MA: Edward Elgar Publishing, 2009), 126.

3. Ibid., 128.

4. Saras Sarasvathy is one of the few entrepreneurship researchers to explicitly recognize the difference between entrepreneurial performance and firm performance and the need to evaluate both. She argues that serial entrepreneurship enables an entrepreneur to learn over time, even through firm failures, and as a result increase the entrepreneur's probability of success (in terms of increased returns and reduced risk) as measured over the course of his career.

5. Noam Wasserman, "The Founder's Dilemma," *Harvard Business Review,* February 2008, 103–9.

6. Noam Wasserman, "Founder Frustrations," blog at http://founderre search.blogspot.com/.

7. Noam Wasserman, "The Founder's Dilemma," http://hbr.org/product/ the-founder-s-dilemma/an/R0802G-PDF-ENG.

8. "New research shows that the trend [of rapidly rising standards in virtually every domain] is continuing, even in realms where the standard already seems impressively high. For example, a cleverly designed study of world championship games in chess found recently that the game is being played at a far higher level today than it was in the nineteenth century, when the world championship was first contested. Using powerful chess software, the researchers found that former champions made many more tactical errors than today's players do. In fact, the champions of yore would match today's players who are just below the master level, not even approaching the grand master or champion levels. The researchers concluded, 'these results imply dramatic improvements at the highest level of intellectual achievement in the game of chess over the last two centuries.' Again, the game hasn't changed, and not enough time has passed for human brains to have changed. What has changed is that people are doing much more with what they've got." Geoff Colvin, *Talent Is Overrated* (New York: The Penguin Group, 2008), 10.

9. R. G. McGrath, "Falling Forward: Real Options Reasoning and Entrepreneurial Failure," *Academy of Management Review* 24, no. 1 (1999): 20.

Chapter 7

1. We contrast these three development strategies—performance-enhancement, incubation, and selective attraction—to the traditional three-legged stool of attraction, retention, and creation used in economic development. The latter triplet is viewed as a convenient categorization by agencies of customers (consumers), but it does not focus on what must be done to help the entrepreneurs and enterprises achieve success. For example, in our framework, both incubation and performance-enhancement efforts can be directed toward *both* existing firms and startups. For an introduction to these ideas see G. A. Lichtenstein and T. S. Lyons, "Managing the Community's Pipeline of Entrepreneurs and Enterprises: A New Way of Thinking about Business Assets," *Economic Development Quarterly* 20, no. 4 (2006): 377–86.

2. The GE Workout is a process pioneered by General Electric in the 1980s to bring together a cross-functional group of people closest to the work to create actionable recommendations for addressing a major business challenge. Implementation is to be achieved in 90 days.

3. The criterion for a financial sale of an asset is any purchaser willing to pay the price the owner sets. The criterion for a strategic sale is a purchaser who would gain some sort of strategic advantage by owning the asset. The purchase of a key supplier by a major manufacturer would be considered a strategic purchase.

4. Building entrepreneurial skills by adding to or changing the team requires a process of transformation by collaboration. In other words, the original entrepreneur or owner must learn to collaborate with the members of a team—to interact as equals, to defer to the individual with the greatest expertise, to delegate where appropriate or even abdicate certain roles, such as would occur if the entrepreneur were to choose to become an employee within the company (such as assuming the position of chief technology officer, under the CEO). Other options are possible as well.

5. This means transition of ownership of the business through succession within the family, to employees, to management, or to entirely new ownership.

6. While franchising is listed here as a selective attraction strategy, in another form it can be considered an incubation strategy. For example, franchising represents a market opportunity for certain types of entrepreneurs in low-income communities to obtain and grow a business asset, and therefore it can be a useful incubation strategy, particularly given its tremendously high success rate. It is an effective but not a particularly developmental opportunity for entrepreneurs who already possess the relevant skills, but it can be a transformational opportunity for those entrepreneurs who need to develop their skills in order to succeed. The limitation of franchising is that the very structure and routine that insures business success rarely provides the type of conditions that enable entrepreneurs to develop skills capable of being used beyond that particular operation (because they only learn to copy these behaviors, not develop skill in producing them).

7. Given the popularity of the concepts of *The Rise of the Creative Class* by Richard Florida (New York: Basic Books, 2003), this is not an unreasonable idea.

8. We have conducted formal analyses of the service providers in a number of communities and regions around the country and sorted them by the segment of the pipeline with which they work.

9. "Economic development programs are not designed and implemented in ways that can achieve their goals, principally because of important political forces. Administrators must run a program to garner support of legislators, a governor, and opinion leaders for program survival. State and locally elected officials need economic development programs to deliver quick, visible projects in their efforts to solve their districts' economic problems, manage business climate politics, and achieve other aims. Achieving implicit goals means that, only occasionally undertaking activities likely to achieve explicit goals."

M. E. Dewar, "Why State and Local Economic Development Programs Cause So Little Economic Development," *Economic Development Quarterly* 12, no. 1 (1998): 68.

10. National Business Incubation Association, *State of the Industry Survey* (Athens, OH: National Business Incubation Association, 2002), 46.

11. Lichtenstein and Lyons, "Managing the Community's Pipeline."

12. The length of time required for particular strategies to yield a desired result is very difficult to estimate. Much depends on the level/stage at which the entrepreneur and enterprise is operating.

13. A cost-benefit ratio.

14. See M. Pastor Jr., P. Dreier, J. E. Grigsby III, and M. López-Garza, *Regions That Work: How Cities and Suburbs Can Grow Together* (Minneapolis: University of Minnesota Press, 2000).

15. This criterion implicates the growing subject of the triple bottom line and attempts to encourage the formation of environmentally beneficial businesses.

16. These standards are the functional equivalent of benchmarking.

Chapter 8

1. According to Saras Sarasvathy, "Headd (2003) found that about a third of closed businesses were successful at closure." Saras D. Sarasvathy, *Effectuation: Elements of Entrepreneurial Expertise* (Northampton, MA: Edward Elgar Publishing, 2009), 122.

2. We have developed and have been successfully utilizing a skills assessment tool for several years for just such a purpose.

3. T. Bates, "Why Do Minority Business Development Programs Generate So Little Minority Business Development?" *Economic Development Quarterly* 9, no. 1 (1995): 2–14; L. J. Servon and T. Bates, "Microenterprise as an Exit Route from Poverty: Recommendations for Programs and Policy Makers," *Journal of Urban Affairs* 20, no. 4 (1998): 419–41; G. A. Lichtenstein, T. S. Lyons, and N. Kutzhanova, "Building Entrepreneurial Communities: The Appropriate Role of Enterprise Development Activities," *Journal of the Community Development Society* 35, no. 1 (2004): 5–24.

4. A. V. Bhide, *The Origin and Evolution of New Businesses* (Oxford: Oxford University Press, 2000), 145.

5. See S. H. Haeckel, *Adaptive Enterprise: Creating and Leading Sense-and-Respond Organizations* (Cambridge, MA: Harvard Business School Press, 1999).

6. Rita G. McGrath, "Falling Forward: Real Options Reasoning and Entrepreneurial Failure," *Academy of Management Review* 24, no. 1 (1999): 24.

7. See E. E. Malizia, "Improving Creation Strategies: Tracking Gazelles in Georgia," *Economic Development Review* 16, no. 3 (1999): 9–11; see also National Commission on Entrepreneurship, *High-Growth Companies: Mapping America's Entrepreneurial Landscape* (Washington, D.C.: National Commission on Entrepreneurship, July 2001).

8. Barbara Miracle, "'Economic Gardening' Is New Buzz Term," *Florida Trend*, November 1, 2009, http://www.floridatrend.com/.

9. PeerSpectives Roundtables are facilitated sessions of 10 to 12 individuals from noncompeting companies that provide a format for sharing experiences instead of giving advice.

10. This information was obtained through personal conversations with local venture capitalists and with participants at the Community Development Venture Capital Alliance conference in Baltimore, Maryland, 1997.

11. This information was obtained through personal conversations with local venture capitalists and participants at Community Development Venture Capital Alliance conference in Baltimore, 1997, as well as private sector venture capitalists in several cities. This assumption may be true, given the amount of money they seek to invest and the rate of return they find acceptable; however, they fail to recognize that investment at lower levels of development is the only way to build a Pipeline to Triple A companies. They should be collaborating with other capital providers to make this happen.

12. Information obtained through personal conversations by one of the authors with over two dozen high-tech entrepreneurs in this northeast U.S. city. This is also true of efforts by venture firms to work in the inner city (so-called community development venture capital). Often the firms they invest in are forced to leave the city—at the request of their new investors in their desire to have them operate out of a better location.

13. Most venture capitalists advise their clients closely and serve on their boards, even calling what they do mentoring. However, it is rare that much time is spent in fact developing the skills of the entrepreneur, as compared to refining them.

14. Many farmers simply did not want others to know their worth. Others didn't understand the importance of that information—a typical Rookie entrepreneur response.

15. Many regions have begun to examine this issue. However, very little of their work is grounded in any kind of analysis of market demand. This is an issue we have done a great deal of work on. Space does not permit us to address it here.

16. See Chris Zook, *Beyond the Core: Expand Your Market without Abandoning Your Roots* (Boston: Harvard Business Press, 2004).

17. We are wandering here into the domain of microenterprise programs. We will not try to review the extensive literature and experience that exists on this subject in this section, but rather raise some questions and provide a different perspective on these issues. We highly recommend that someone examine this literature using the Pipeline framework.

18. This can be done by extending the skills assessment into this population segment.

19. Using a skills assessment tool would be more cost-effective than simply accepting all possible clients and seeing who succeeds or fails at the end of the program.

20. Accurate data are crucial to being able to draw the proper conclusions and make the right decisions. Since secondary data is not captured according

to Pipeline criteria, we have developed tools to enable data collection on this basis. Among these is a tool for measuring entrepreneurship skills and another for profiling companies at each stage in the business life cycle.

Chapter 9

1. Scott Shane, *The Illusions of Entrepreneurship* (New Haven, CT: Yale University Press, 2008), 164.

2. There are clearly some efficiencies to be gained from a larger deal in terms of transaction costs. It would take more than six deals to earn the same return in absolute dollars. But that is not the point of this example. Our question is about what makes one deal better in relative terms. It could also be the case that there are benefits to be gained from six smaller deals over one larger deal, in terms of risk reduction, a greater number of opportunities to be explored, and equity considerations, such as a broader distribution of wealth and jobs.

3. Skill levels greatly influence the potential for success and the measurement of entrepreneurial risk. All other things being equal, the probability of success is increased the higher the skill level. Therefore, the lower the skill level, the higher the risk and the greater probability of failure. Also, the greater the disparity between an entrepreneur's skill level and the skill level required to effectively capture that opportunity, the greater the risk of failure.

4. One way to underwrite the risk would be to differentiate the terms of a financial transaction (e.g., interest rate, payback period, penalties, and the proactive encouragement to get support in the form of coaching or technical assistance), based on the assessed skill level of the entrepreneur.

5. Amar Bhide and Carl Schramm, "Phelps's Prize," *Wall Street Journal,* January 29, 2007, http://online.wsj.com/article/SB117003072952090648.html.

6. William A. Sahlman, "How to Write a Great Business Plan," *Harvard Business Review,* July–August 1997, 101.

7. This challenge of matching requires an assessment of skill level of the entrepreneur as well as an in-depth analysis of the skill level required by the opportunity. We have designed tools for both tasks.

8. Nor does it invest in the process of developing an opportunity; they must already be well formed and developed.

9. See Burton H. Klein, *Dynamic Economics* (Cambridge, MA: Harvard University Press, 1977); this statement has been confirmed by numerous other studies.

10. Saras D. Sarasvathy, *Effectuation: Elements of Entrepreneurial Expertise* (Northampton, MA: Edward Elgar Publishing, 2009), 179–80.

11. Sarasvathy, *Effectuation,* 180–81.

12. The assumption of responsibility for the community's Pipeline is a major issue to which we continue to give considerable thought. While the subject is much too complex to cover here, our field experience tells us that individual governments or enterprise development service provider organizations

are not well suited for the task. More promising are covenantal relationships among multiple regional stakeholder organizations, similar to those used in this country's colonial era to provide public services.

13. See Erik Pages, Robert Albright, and Rural EDS Partners, *Hello My Business Name Is . . . A Guide to Building Entrepreneurial Networks in North Carolina* (Durham, NC: Council for Entrepreneurial Development, 2006).

14. Jonathan Ortmans is a senior fellow at the Kauffman Foundation. See "Rockstar Entrepreneurs Don't Come to Washington," http://www.entrepre neurship.org/PolicyForum/Blog/post/2009/09/28/Rockstar-Entrepre neurs-Dont-Come-to-Washington.aspx. "Evidence shows entrepreneurs have not had an influence on economic policy that is measurable to their role as drivers of economic growth."

15. This stands in contrast to standard portfolio theory in finance, whose objective is to diversify risk among intentionally unrelated investments.

16. See G. A. Lichtenstein and T. S. Lyons, "The Entrepreneurial Development System: Transforming Business Talent and Community Economies," *Economic Development Quarterly* 15, no. 1 (2001): 3–20.

17. R. G. McGrath, "Falling Forward: Real Options Reasoning and Entrepreneurial Failure," *Academy of Management Review* 24, no. 1 (1999): 16.

18. We frequently remind people that drug dealers are often skilled in network marketing and financial management. Asking them to exchange their lucrative business for a minimum wage job is a nonstarter. But offering them a chance to own and operate a legitimate enterprise that utilizes those skills and gives them the opportunity to make as much, if not more, money is a deal worthy of their consideration. The incentives we offer must be equal to the ambition being demonstrated. Similarly, how many troublemakers in our communities and schools, such as gang leaders or dropouts, are really intelligent individuals who are not challenged by the education system? What would happen if we offered them new opportunities toward which to direct their energies? If we are going to make matches, let's define entrepreneurial skills more broadly to include everyone.

19. See G. P. Sweeney, *Innovation, Entrepreneurs and Regional Development* (New York: St. Martin's Press, 1987).

20. See G. A. Lichtenstein, T. S. Lyons, and N. Kutzhanova, "Building Entrepreneurial Communities: The Appropriate Role of Enterprise Development Activities," *Journal of the Community Development Society* 35, no. 1 (2004): 5–24.

21. C. M. Christensen and M. E. Raynor, *The Innovator's Solution* (Cambridge, MA: Harvard Business School Press, 2003), 246.

22. Dees, Emerson, and Economy provide a useful frame for thinking about the inevitable resistance that radical innovations encounter. They identify two major types of resistance: threat-based resistance and inertia-based resistance. They also discuss three major types of threats that are most likely to induce resistance: threat to competence, threat by competition and threat to core values. J. Gregory Dees, Jed Emerson, and Peter Economy, *Enterprising Nonprofits: A Toolkit for Social Entrepreneurs* (New York: Wiley, 2001).

23. See Everett M. Rogers, *Diffusion of Innovations*, 4th ed. (New York: The Free Press, 1995).

24. See Lloyd E. Shefsky, *Entrepreneurs Are Made Not Born* (New York: McGraw-Hill, 1996).

25. See T. S. Lyons, G. A. Lichtenstein, and N. Kutzhanova, "What Makes a Successful Entrepreneur?" in *Entrepreneurship and Local Economic Development*, ed. Norman Walzer, 103–24 (Lanham, MD: Lexington Books, 2007).

26. See Lichtenstein, Lyons, and Kutzhanova, "Building Entrepreneurial Communities"; and D. DeFaoite, C. Henry, K. Johnston, and P. van der Sijde, "Education and Training for Entrepreneurs: A Consideration of Initiatives in Ireland and the Netherlands," *Education and Training* 45, nos. 8–9 (2003): 430–38.

27. See C. Henry, F. Hill, and C. Leitch, "Developing a Coherent Enterprise Support Policy: A New Challenge for Government," *Planning and Environment C: Government and Policy* 21, no. 1 (2003): 3–19.

Selected Bibliography

Abbott, Edwin A. *Flatland: Romance of Many Dimensions*, 5th ed. New York: HarperCollins, 1963.

Argyris, Chris, Robert Putnam, and Diane McLain Smith. *Action Science*. San Francisco: Jossey-Bass Publishers, 1985.

Autere, J.E.A. "Is Entrepreneurship Learned? Influence of Mental Models on Growth Motivation, Strategy, and Growth." Working Paper Series 2000/7. Espo, Finland: Institute of Strategy and International Business.

Bates, T. "Why Do Minority Business Development Programs Generate So Little Minority Business Development?" *Economic Development Quarterly* 9, no. 1 (1995): 2–14.

Begley, T.M., and D. P. Boyd. "Psychological Characteristics Associated with Performance in Entrepreneurial Firms and Smaller Businesses." *Journal of Business Venturing* 2, no. 1 (1987): 79–93.

Bhide, A. V. *The Origin and Evolution of New Businesses*. Oxford: Oxford University Press, 2000.

Bhide, Amar, and Carl Schramm. "Phelps's Prize." *Wall Street Journal*, January 29, 2007, http://online.wsj.com/article/SB117003072952090648.html.

Birch, D. *The Job Generation Process*. Cambridge, MA: MIT Program on Neighborhood and Regional Change, 1979.

Bourdieu, P. *Outline of a Theory of Practice*. Cambridge: Cambridge University Press, 1990.

Bourdieu, P., and L.D.C. Wacquant. *An Invitation to a Reflexive Sociology*. Chicago: University of Chicago Press, 1992.

Brockhaus, R. H. Sr. "Risk Taking Propensity of Entrepreneurs." *Academy of Management Journal* 23 (1980): 509–20.

Brockhaus, R. H. Sr., and P. S. Horwitz. "The Psychology of the Entrepreneur." In *The Art and Science of Entrepreneurship*, edited by D. L. Sexton and R. W. Smilor, 25–48. Cambridge, MA: Ballinger, 1986.

Burrows, P., and J. Greene, "Yes, Steve, You Fixed It. Congrats! Now What's Act Two?" *BusinessWeek*, July 31, 2000, cover story.

Cammann, Cortlandt. "Action Usable Knowledge." In *Exploring Clinical Methods for Social Research*, edited by David N. Berg and Kenwyn K. Smith, 115. Beverly Hills, CA: Sage Publications, 1985.

Case, J. "A Study of Gazelles by Cognetics." *Inc. Magazine*, May 2001.

Christensen, C. M., and M. E. Raynor. *The Innovator's Solution*. Cambridge, MA: Harvard Business School Press, 2003.

Clifford, Stephanie. "Never Listen to Céline? Radio Meter Begs to Differ." *New York Times*, December 16, 2009.

Colvin, Geoff. *Talent Is Overrated*. New York: The Penguin Group, 2008.

Cooper, A. C., and W. C. Dunkelberg. "Entrepreneurial Research: Old Questions, New Answers, and Methodological Issues." *American Journal of Small Business* 11, no. 3 (1987): 1–20.

Corning, Peter A. *Holistic Darwinism*. Chicago: University of Chicago Press, 2005.

Coyle, Daniel. *The Talent Code*. New York: Bantam, 2009.

Dees, J. Gregory, Jed Emerson, and Peter Economy. *Enterprising Nonprofits: A Toolkit for Social Entrepreneurs*. New York: Wiley, 2001.

DeFaoite, D., C. Henry, K. Johnston, and P. van der Sijde. "Education and Training for Entrepreneurs: A Consideration of Initiatives in Ireland and the Netherlands." *Education and Training* 45, nos. 8–9 (2003): 430–38.

Dewar, M. E. "Why State and Local Economic Development Programs Cause So Little Economic Development." *Economic Development Quarterly* 12, no. 1 (1998): 68–87.

Dyck, B., M. Mauws, F. A. Starke, and G. A. Mischke. "Passing the Baton: The Importance of Sequence, Timing, Technique and Communication in Executive Succession." *Journal of Business Venturing* 17 (2002): 143–62.

Evans, G. Heberton Jr. "A Century of Entrepreneurship in the United States with Emphases upon Large Manufacturing Concerns." *Explorations in Entrepreneurial History* 10, no. 2 (1957): 90–103.

Florida, Richard. *The Rise of the Creative Class: And How It's Transforming Work, Leisure, Community and Everyday Life*. New York: Basic Books, 2003.

Gerber, M. E. *The E-Myth Revisited: Why Most Small Businesses Don't Work and What to do About It*. New York: HarperCollins, 1995.

Gilmore, J. H., and B. J. Pine II. "Beyond Goods and Services." *Strategy & Leadership*, May/June 1997, 11–17.

Gladwell, Malcolm. *Outliers*. New York: Little, Brown and Company, 2008.

Globalsecurity.org, November 30, 2004, http://www.globalsecurity.org/military/intro/ranks.htm.

Goleman, Daniel. *Emotional Intelligence*. New York: Bantam Books, 1995.

Gunderson, Gerald. *The Wealth Creators: An Entrepreneurial History of the United States*. New York: Penguin Books, 1990.

Haeckel, S. H. *Adaptive Enterprise: Creating and Leading Sense-and-Respond Organizations*. Cambridge, MA: Harvard Business School Press, 1999.

Hamlin, R. E., and T. S. Lyons. *Financing Small Business in America: Debt Capital in the Global Economy*. Westport, CT: Praeger, 2003.

Hashikawa, Kenryu. *Rural Entrepreneurship in New Jersey during the Early Republic*. Ph.D. Diss. Columbia University, New York, 2002.

Headd, B. "Redefining Business Success: Distinguishing between Closure and Failure." *Small Business Economics* 21 (2003): 51–61.

Henry, C., F. Hill, and C. Leitch. "Developing a Coherent Enterprise Support Policy: A New Challenge for Government." *Planning and Environment C: Government and Policy* 21, no. 1 (2003): 3–19.

Hornaday, J. A., and J. Aboud. "Characteristics of Successful Entrepreneurs." *Personnel Psychology* 24 (1971): 141–53.

Hull, D. L., J. J. Bosley, and G. G. Udell. "Renewing the Hunt for the Heffalump: Identifying Potential Entrepreneurs by Personality Characteristics." *Journal of Business Management* 20, no. 2 (1982): 11–19.

Kassicieh, S. K., H. R. Radosevich, and C. M. Banbury. "Using Attitudinal, Situational, and Personal Characteristics Variables to Predict Future Entrepreneurs from National Laboratory Inventors." *IEEE Transactions on Engineering Management* 44 (1997): 248–57.

Kegan, Robert, and Lisa Laskow Lahey. *Immunity to Change.* Cambridge, MA: Harvard Business Press, 2009.

Kirchhoff, Bruce A. *Entrepreneurship and Dynamic Capitalism: The Economics of Business Firm Formation and Growth.* Westport, CT: Praeger Publishers, 1994.

Klein, Burton H. *Dynamic Economics.* Cambridge, MA: Harvard University Press, 1977.

Klein, Burton H. *Prices, Wages and Business Cycles: A Dynamic Theory.* Elmsford, NY: Pergamon Press, 1984.

Kutzhanova, Nailya, Thomas S. Lyons, and Gregg A. Lichtenstein. "Skill-Based Development of Entrepreneurs and the Role of Personal and Peer Group Coaching in Enterprise Development." *Economic Development Quarterly* 23, no. 3, August 2009.

Lewin, Kurt. *Field Theory in Social Science.* New York: Harpers & Brothers Publishing, 1951.

Lichtenstein, Gregg A. "The Significance of Relationships in Entrepreneurship: A Case Study of the Ecology of Enterprise in Two Business Incubators." PhD diss., University of Pennsylvania, 1992.

Lichtenstein, Gregg A., and T. S. Lyons. "The Entrepreneurial Development System: Transforming Business Talent and Community Economies." *Economic Development Quarterly* 15, no. 1 (2001): 3–20.

Lichtenstein, Gregg A., and T. S. Lyons. *Incubating New Enterprises: A Guide to Successful Practice.* Washington, DC: The Aspen Institute, 1996.

Lichtenstein, Gregg A., and T. S. Lyons. "Managing the Community's Pipeline of Entrepreneurs and Enterprises: A New Way of Thinking about Business Assets." *Economic Development Quarterly* 20, no. 4 (2006): 377–86.

Lichtenstein, Gregg A., and Thomas S. Lyons. "Revisiting the Business Life-Cycle: Proposing an Actionable Model for Assessing and Fostering Entrepreneurship." *International Journal of Entrepreneurship and Innovation* 9, no. 4 (2008): 241–50.

Lichtenstein, Gregg A., T. S. Lyons, and N. Kutzhanova. "Building Entrepreneurial Communities: the Appropriate Role of Enterprise Development Activities." *Journal of the Community Development Society* 35, no. 1 (2004): 5–24.

Longenecker, J. G., C. W. Moore, J. W. Petty, and L. E. Palich. *Small Business Management: An Entrepreneurial Emphasis,* 13th ed. Mason, OH: Thomson South-Western, 2006.

Loveridge, Scott, and Denys Nizalov. "Operationalizing the Entrepreneurial Pipeline Theory: An Empirical Assessment of the Optimal Size Distribution of Local Firms." *Economic Development Quarterly* 21, no. 3 (2007): 244–62.

Lyons, Thomas, S., Gregg A. Lichtenstein, and Nailya Kutzhanova. "What Makes a Successful Entrepreneur?" In *Entrepreneurship and Local Economic Development,* edited by Norman Walzer, 103–24. Lanham, MD: Lexington Books, 2007.

Major League Baseball Players Association, http://mlbplayers.mlb.com/pa/index.jsp.

Malizia, E. E. "Improving Creation Strategies: Tracking Gazelles in Georgia." *Economic Development Review* 16, no. 3 (1999): 9–11.

Markley, Deborah, Don Macke, and Vicki B. Luther. *Energizing Entrepreneurs: Charting a Course for Rural Communities.* Lincoln, NE: RUPRI Center for Rural Entrepreneurship and Heartland Center for Leadership Development, 2005.

McClelland, D. C., J. W. Atkinson, R. A. Clark, and E. L. Lowell. *The Achievement Motive.* New York: Appleton-Century-Crofts, 1953.

McGrath, R. G. "Falling Forward: Real Options Reasoning and Entrepreneurial Failure." *Academy of Management Review* 24, no. 1 (1999): 13–30.

McGrath, Rita Gunther, and Ian C. MacMillan. *Discovery-Driven Growth.* Cambridge, MA: Harvard Business Press, 2009.

Midgette, Anne. "The End of the Great Big American Voice." *New York Times,* November 13, 2005.

Miracle, Barbara, "'Economic Gardening' Is New Buzz Term." *Florida Trend,* November 1, 2009, http://www.floridatrend.com/.

Moore, G. A. *Dealing with Darwin.* New York: Penguin Group, 2005.

Morgan, Kevin. "The Exaggerated Death of Geography: Learning, Proximity and Territorial Innovation Systems." *Journal of Economic Geography* 4 (2004): 3–21.

National Business Incubation Association. *State of the Industry Survey.* Athens, OH: National Business Incubation Association, 2002.

National Commission on Entrepreneurship. *High-Growth Companies: Mapping America's Entrepreneurial Landscape.* Washington, DC: National Commission on Entrepreneurship, July 2001.

Ortmans, Jonathan. "Rockstar Entrepreneurs Don't Come to Washington." *Kauffman Foundation,* http://www.entrepreneurship.org/PolicyForum/Blog/post/2009/09/28/Rockstar-Entrepreneurs-Dont-Come-to-Washington.aspx.

Pages, Erik, Robert Albright, and Rural EDS Partners. *Hello My Business Name Is . . . A Guide to Building Entrepreneurial Networks in North Carolina.* Durham, NC: Council for Entrepreneurial Development, 2006.

Pastor, M. Jr., P. Dreier, J. E. Grigsby III, and M. López-Garza. *Regions That Work: How Cities and Suburbs Can Grow Together.* Minneapolis: University of Minnesota Press, 2000.

Pine, B. J. II, and J. H. Gilmore. *The Experience Economy.* Boston: Harvard Business School Press, 1999.

Pozen, D. "We Are All Entrepreneurs Now." *Wake Forest Law Review* 43, no. 1 (2008).

Rauch, A., and M. Frese. "Psychological Approaches to Entrepreneurial Success: A General Model and an Overview of Findings." In *International Review of Industrial and Organizational Psychology*, edited by C. L. Cooper and I. T. Robertson, 100–42. Chichester, Sussex, UK: Wiley & Sons, 2000.

Reynolds, Paul D., Nancy M. Carter, William B. Gartner, and Patricia G. Greene. "The Prevalence of Nascent Entrepreneurs in the United States: Evidence from the Panel Study of Entrepreneurial Dynamics." *Small Business Economics* 23 (2004): 263–84.

Rogers, Everett M. *Diffusion of Innovations*, 4th ed. New York: The Free Press, 1995.

Rotter, J. B. "Generalized Expectancies for Internal versus External Control of Reinforcement." *Psychological Monographs* 80, no. 1 (1966): 1–28.

Sahlman, William A. "How to Write a Great Business Plan." *Harvard Business Review*, July–August, 1997.

Sarasvathy, Saras D. *Effectuation: Elements of Entrepreneurial Expertise.* Northampton, MA: Edward Elgar Publishing, 2009.

Schon, D. A. *Educating the Reflective Practitioner.* San Francisco: Jossey-Bass, 1987.

Schon, D. A. *The Reflective Practitioner.* New York: Basic Books, 1983.

Schumpeter, Joseph A. *The Theory of Economic Development.* New Brunswick, NJ: Transaction Publishers, 1983.

Servon, L. J., and T. Bates. "Microenterprise as an Exit Route from Poverty: Recommendations for Programs and Policy Makers." *Journal of Urban Affairs* 20, no. 4 (1998): 419–41.

Shane, Scott. *The Illusions of Entrepreneurship.* New Haven, CT: Yale University Press, 2008.

Shefsky, Lloyd E. *Entrepreneurs Are Made Not Born.* New York: McGraw-Hill, 1996.

Souman, Jan L., Ilja Frissen, Manish N. Sreenivasa, and Marc O. Ernst. "Walking Straight into Circles." *Current Biology* 19, no. 18 (2009): 1538–42.

Sweeney, G. P. *Innovation, Entrepreneurs and Regional Development.* New York: St. Martin's Press, 1987.

Timmons, J., L. Smollen, and A. Dingee. *New Venture Creation: A Guide to Entrepreneurship.* Hamate, IL: Irwin, 1985.

Timmons, J. A., and S. Spinelli. *New Venture Creation: Entrepreneurship for the 21st Century.* Boston: McGraw-Hill Irwin, 2007.

Torbert, William R. *The Balance of Power, Transforming Self, Society, and Scientific Inquiry.* Newbury Park, CA: Sage Publications, 1991.

Torre, Pablo S. "How (and Why) Athletes Go Broke," March 23, 2009, http://sportsillustrated.cnn.com/vault/article/magazine/MAG1153364/index/index.htm.

Warner, Sam Bass Jr. *The Private City: Philadelphia in Three Periods of Its Growth*, 2nd ed. Philadelphia: University of Pennsylvania Press, 1987.

Wasserman, Noam. "Founder Frustrations," blog at http://founderresearch. blogspot.com/.

Wasserman, Noam. "The Founder's Dilemma." *Harvard Business Review*, February 2008.

Wasserman, Noam. The Founder's Dilemma, http://hbr.org/product/the-founder-s-dilemma/an/R0802G-PDF-ENG.

Westhead, P., C. Howorth, and M. Cowling. "Ownership and Management Issues in First Generation and Multi-Generation Family Firms." *Entrepreneurship and Regional Development* 14 (2002): 247–69.

Whyte, W. F. "On the Uses of Social Science Research." *American Sociological Review* 51 (1986): 555–63.

Whyte, W. F., D. J. Greenwood, and P. Lazes. "Participatory Action Research: Through Practice to Science in Social Research." In *Participatory Action Research*, edited by W. F. Whyte, 19–55. Newbury Park, CA: Sage Publications, 1991.

Zlotin, Boris, and Alla Zusman. *Levels of Invention and Intellectual Property Strategies*. Southfield, MI: Ideation International, 2003.

Zook, Chris. *Beyond the Core: Expand Your Market without Abandoning Your Roots*. Boston: Harvard Business Press, 2004.

Index

About the Authors

GREGG A. LICHTENSTEIN is the president of Collaborative Strategies, LLC, a 20-year-old firm that specializes in working with entrepreneurs, intrapreneurs, and strategic alliances. In addition to having received a Ph.D. from the Wharton School in entrepreneurship and social systems sciences, he is and continues to be an entrepreneur—having started and led several technology ventures. Dr. Lichtenstein has published widely on entrepreneurship in academic and popular business outlets. Along with his colleague Dr. Thomas Lyons, he authored the first comprehensive reference on working with startups—*Incubating New Enterprises,* published by the Aspen Institute, which has also been translated into Spanish and published in South America. In addition, he and Dr. Lyons have designed the Entrepreneurial League System® (ELS), a business that specializes in coaching entrepreneurs. Dr. Lichtenstein is responsible for implementing the ELS in several regions around the world.

THOMAS S. LYONS is the Lawrence N. Field Family Chair in Entrepreneurship and a professor of management in the Zicklin School of Business at Baruch College of the City University of New York. Among his other duties at Baruch, he is a mentor to entrepreneurs who are clients of the Field Center for Entrepreneurship and to student teams in the annual business plan competition. Dr. Lyons has served on the boards of directors or advisory boards of several nonprofit enterprise development organizations. He is a former entrepreneur and a former local economic development planner. He has coauthored nine books on the subjects of economic development and entrepreneurship, including *Creating an Economic Development Action Plan, Incubating New Enterprises, Economy without Walls, and Economic Development: Strategies for State and Local Practice.* He holds a Ph.D. in urban and regional planning from the University of Michigan at Ann Arbor.

For more information about our activities in this area, please visit our Web sites: http://www.investinginentrepreneurs.com and http://www.pipelineofentrepreneurs.com.